Teacher's Classroom Guide
To Robert Stanek's Magic Lands: Into the Beyond

Teacher's Classroom Guide
To Robert Stanek's Magic Lands:
Journey Beyond the Beyond
Based on the novel written by Robert Stanek

Copyright © 2005 by Robert Stanek
Copyright © 2005 by Reagent Press

All rights reserved, including the right to reproduce this book, or portions thereof, in any form. Printed in the United States of America.

Reagent Press
Published by Virtual Press, Inc.

Cover design & illustration by Reagent Press
ISBN 1-57545-034-8

Reagent Press grants classroom teachers the right to reproduce copies of materials from Exploring Magic Lands in the Classroom, Review Questions for Discussion, Quizzes, Post-Reading Activities, and Culminating Project sections of this book for classroom use only. No other part of this publication may be reproduced in whole or in part.

The reproduction of any part for an entire school or school system is strictly prohibited. No part of this publication may be transmitted, stored, or recorded in any form without written permission from the publisher.

CONTENTS

BEFORE READING 9

About Robert Stanek 10

Introduction 11
    Summary   11
    Story Characters   12
    Book Connections   12

Exploring *Magic Lands* in the Classroom 13

Expanding Vocabulary 14
    Vocabulary for Chapters 1-3   15
    Vocabulary for Chapters 4-6   16
    Vocabulary for Chapters 7-9   17
    Vocabulary for Chapters 10-12   18

Learning Creatively 19

AN INTERVIEW WITH ROBERT STANEK 21

Family and Childhood 22
    How many brothers and sisters do you have?   22
    Did bullies ever pick on you?   22
    Tell me about your Big Brother.   22
    Did you read a lot when you were a child?   23
    Did you want to be a writer back then?   24
    Did you have any pets when you were little?   24

Tell us about your father and mother.   25
Did you always do as you were told?   26
Tell us about your grandparents.   26
Why did you move to the country? 27
Tell us about the farmhouse and growing up in the country.   28
What else do you remember about living there?   28
What was it like not having your father in your life?   29

School Days **30**

Tell me about your first school.   30
Tell me about your walks to school.   30
What do you remember about that school?   31
Tell us about moving and changing schools.   32
Who was your favorite teacher?   33
Was there anything you didn't like about school? 34
Outside of school, what was your childhood like? 36
Have you ever gone back to the schools you attended?   36
Did you really get leeches all over you one time?   37
Did you watch a lot of television?   37
Do you miss those times?   38
A car hit you when you were young. What happened?   38

Military Career **40**

Why did you join the military?   40
What do you remember about basic training?   41
Was language school hard?   42
Where did you go next?   43
Did you like living in Texas?   44
Tell me about your first assignment.   44
Did training end once you got to your first assignment?   45
Did you travel in Japan?   46
Did you learn Japanese?   47

Did you study martial arts? 47
Where did you go after Japan? 48
Was survival school really scary? 48
Is it true you met your wife while going to flying school? 50
What was Germany like? 50
Tell me more about the food in Europe. 51
Did you travel in Europe? 51
How come you had to go to war? 52
Was it scary? 52
Tell me about Hawaii. 53
What made you want to get a degree, finally? 54
Why did you leave the military? 55

Writing Career 56
When did you first start writing fiction? 56
When did you first try to get published? 57
What happened after your first book was published? 58
What is *Magic Lands* about? 59
What about the imagery in the story? 59
Prejudice and preconception seem to be themes in your work. 59
Tell us about the bulls and the slithers. 60
Are other *Magic Lands* books planned? 60

REVIEW QUESTIONS 61

Review Questions for Discussion: Chapter 1 62

Review Questions for Discussion: Chapters 2-3 63

Chapter 2 63

Chapter 3 63

Review Questions for Discussion: Chapters 4-5 64

Chapter 4 64

Chapter 5 64

Review Questions for Discussion: Chapters 6-7 65

Chapter 6 65

Chapter 7 65

Review Questions for Discussion: Chapters 8-9 66

Chapter 8 66

Chapter 9 66

Review Questions for Discussion: Chapters 10-11 67

Chapter 10 67

Chapter 11 67

Review Questions for Discussion: Chapter 12 68

QUIZZES 69

Quiz!: Chapter 1 70

Quiz!: Chapter 2 71

Quiz!: Chapter 3 72

Quiz!: Chapter 4 73

Quiz!: Chapter 5 74

Quiz!: Chapter 6 75

Quiz!: Chapter 7 76

Quiz!: Chapter 8 77

Quiz!: Chapter 9 78

Quiz!: Chapter 10 79

Quiz!: Chapter 11 80

Quiz!: Chapter 12 81

POST-READING & WRITING ACTIVITIES 83

Write a Journal! 84

What's the main idea? 85

Find the Meaning 86

Put Yourself in Ray's Place 87

What's So Special About Ray's Quest 88

Be the Character! 89

What's in a Personality? 90

All About Friends 91

Ray's Vision Quest 92

Oh no the Palisades! 93

You Choose the Companion! 94

The Place Lost and Deep 95

Friend or Adversary? 96

Into the Beyond 97

CULMINATING PROJECT FOR *MAGIC LANDS* 99
    Section 1   100
    Section 2   101
    Section 3   101

Before Reading

About Robert Stanek

Robert Stanek was born in Burlington, Wisconsin. His father was an entrepreneur who immigrated to America from Budapest, Hungary. His mother is the granddaughter of French and Norwegian immigrants.

Robert became interested in writing as a child and was creating stories virtually from the time he was able to read and write. He started work as a journalist and editor—with a school newspaper—at the age of nine!

He joined the United States Air Force at the age of nineteen and at twenty-six served in the Persian Gulf War. He earned many medals for his wartime service, including the United States of America's highest flying honor, the Air Force Distinguished Flying Cross.

At age thirty-one, he decided to devote most of his time to full-length works of fact and fiction. Since then has written more than fifty books, many of them international best sellers, and his work has been published in more than fifty countries, including the United States, Britain, Japan, Korea, Canada, France, Australia, Germany, India, Spain, Italy, Turkey and various Latin American countries.

Today he works as a full-time author with an interest in, among other things, technology, computers, and the outdoors! He has broadcast and lectured about his work throughout the United States. Recently he has been getting praise for his artwork and the covers he designed for his *Ruin Mist* books. You can learn more about this popular author and artist by visiting the publisher's Web site (http://www.tvpress.com/).

Teacher's Classroom Guide: Before Reading

Introduction

Good books become a part of our lives. The best seem like old friends. They contain words and characters that inspire us. They give us insights and provide new views of our world, and they can do this even if they are themselves windows into entirely new worlds. In *Magic Lands: Journey Beyond the Beyond*, Robert Stanek provides such a window, and readers around the world are discovering and cherishing the book.

Teachers have discovered the book as well. They've learned that the book has a story to tell beyond the typed page. The book is a window into the heart, mind, and soul. It tells a story of self-discovery, friendship, loyalty, and compassion.

Summary

Following the village elder's advice, Ray leaves his home village, setting out for the place lost and deep where he will find a companion for his journey to the stone land and where he will discover that there is no easy path from childhood to manhood. On his journey Ray encounters many strange creatures, including Old Bull and Mother Slither. Old Bull follows and chases Ray most of the journey, and Ray encounters Mother Slither when he least expects it.

Ray's first night away from his home village finds him in the deep—a place far from his home. A misstep causes Ray to fall and that's when he encounters a young bull with snapping jaws, glistening white teeth and a lurching tail. Ray must fight for his life and this leaves him exhausted. This encounter is the first of many on Ray's journey.

Teacher's Classroom Guide: Before Reading

Story Characters

Characters introduced in the story include:

Ray	Youngest son of Waddymarre. He is from Third Village.
Village Smoot	Soothsayer and village elder for Third Village.
Old Bull	Mature bull whose territory Ray must go through.
Mother Slither	Brooding female slither.
Ephramme	One of Ray's friends, a boyhood companion.
Isaac	One of Ray's friends, a boyhood companion.
Keene	One of Ray's friends, a boyhood companion.
Tall	One of Ray's friends, a boyhood companion.
Kerry	Daughter of Stirling and one of the Out.
True	A newly hatched slither.
Waring	Kerry's falkish, a large bird that Kerry can talk with.

These characters have significant parts to play in the books, but they are not the only characters in the books. Other characters you will see include creatures and peoples Ray encounters, including a young bull and a group of outsiders.

Book Connections

Other books by Robert Stanek include:

- *The Kingdoms & the Elves of the Reaches (Keeper Martin's Tales, Books 1-4)*
- *In the Service of Dragons (Keeper Martin's Tales, Books 5-8)*
- *The Elf Queen & the King (Ruin Mist Tales, Books 1-4)*
- *Ruin Mist Heroes, Legends & Beyond*
- *Magic Lands & Other Stories*

Teacher's Classroom Guide: Before Reading

Exploring Magic Lands in the Classroom

Before you begin, you may want to discuss the difference between a fantasy and a realistic novel. Ray's watery world and the Stone Land are imaginary places. Magic is an important part of the story, as it is with most fantasy, including classic fairy tales like Cinderella, Snow White, and even Pinocchio. Magic is what brings Pinocchio to life, and it's what makes Pinocchio's nose grow when he lies.

Then, do some pre-reading activities with the class. Activities that might work well in your class include:

- Ask the students what they think when they hear the words "Magic Lands: Journey Beyond the Beyond." Note their responses and then tell them that is the title of the book they are about to read.
- Find out if your students have heard of Robert Stanek, and if they know anything about his personal life or his writing. You may want to read some of the questions and answers from the section of this text entitled "An Interview with Robert Stanek."
- Have students answer these questions:
  1. Are you interested in:
     - stories of fantasy and magic?
     - struggles between individuals and nature?
     - ways people can change their lives?
     - sacrifices one can make to help others?
  2. Have you ever:
     - wished things were different in your life?
     - gone on a long trip but were unsure about it?
     - regretted a decision that you've made?
     - been afraid to meet someone new?

Teacher's Classroom Guide: Before Reading

Expanding Vocabulary

Like other works of fiction, Robert Stanek's *Magic Lands: Journey Beyond the Beyond* will help expand students' vocabulary. You can help your students learn and retain these words by providing interesting activities.

Activities that you may want to try include:
- Challenge your students to look up new words in the dictionary and write down the meanings after reading each chapter. Have your students alphabetize the words and create a glossary.
- Use new words as part of a weekly vocabulary test, or challenge your students to a weekly vocabulary bee that uses the words in a particular chapter. Ask your students to define the words as well as spell them.
- Give your students the opportunity to practice their writing skills by using the words in sentences and paragraphs. Afterward, have students share their work with the class.
- Play 20 Questions or Vocabulary Charades. With 20 Questions, one student selects a vocabulary word and gives clues about it while other students ask questions and try to guess the word. With Vocabulary Charades, one student selects a vocabulary word and acts it out while other students try to guess the word.

Next, you'll find lists of vocabulary words, organized by chapter. If you find there are too many words or that some of the words are too difficult for a particular chapter, edit the list to make it more appropriate for your students.

Teacher's Classroom Guide: Before Reading

Vocabulary for Chapters 1-3

Chapter 1

Quest	Residence	Baritone
Watchful	Inquire	Perceive
Companion	Impressive	Nimble
Suffice	Gingerly	Respectfully
Encounter	Maneuvering	Mourning

Chapter 2

Invade	Lurching	Excessive
Fatal	Glistened	Oblige
Beleaguered	Unclasp	Acclimate
Trumpeting	Scampering	Abode
Pungent	Instinct	Innumerable
Tedious	Abound	Quarters

Chapter 3

Challenger	Brood	Intent
Exalted	Exception	Reclined
Groomed	Dangerous	Hindrance
Retaliation	Fervent	Imagination
Impulse	Instinct	Mandible
Primal	Adrenaline	Interim
Circumstances	Protective	Willingly

Vocabulary for Chapters 4-6

Chapter 4

Twilight	Slumber	Herald
Rationalize	Subconscious	Phenomenon
Transition	Inspection	Moderate
Guidance	Resistance	Domicile
Prolonged	Renewed	Sojourn
Graceful	Lethargy	Stalwart
Unoccupied	Mischievously	Absently
Countenance	Resonance	Lacerations

Chapter 5

Tempestuous	Precious	Arduous
Obscurity	Encroaching	Rhythmic
Pensive	Somber	Foreboding
Irritated	Abhorrence	Pulsations
Remnants	Precipitation	Leverage
Engagement	Fledgling	Melancholy
Temptation	Sacrifice	Grimace

Chapter 6

Demeanor	Concentration	Disposition
Awestruck	Inclination	Celebration
Etiquette	Rebuttal	Bantam
Elation	Jubilation	Crafty
Lackluster	Determination	Cumbersome
Perspiration	Concealment	Precariously
Precision		

Teacher's Classroom Guide: Before Reading

Vocabulary for Chapters 7-9

Chapter 7

Turbulent	Noble	Preservation
Crucial	Dissipated	Necessitated
Adjourned	Transformation	Burdensome
Troublesome	Recollection	Unprecedented
Venerable	Weathered	Stoic
Precipice	Reverberated	Cataclysmic
Revelation	Aspirations	Appropriate

Chapter 8

Incident	Drudgery	Diffident
Edifice	Absence	Meandering
Steadfastness	Self-implemented	Yearnings
Secluded	Strategically	Erosion
Proportioned	Purposeful	Spectacle
Remorse		

Chapter 9

Premonition	Persistent	Perception
Contradictions	Adorning	Testaments
Camouflage	Ominous	Apprehension
Impression	Overcompensated	Disparity

Vocabulary for Chapters 10-12

Chapter 10

Sensation	Contrary	Disappearance
Jeopardy	Curious	Conveyed
Craving	Vibration	Vibrancy
Indication	Enlighten	Registered

Chapter 11

Embroidered	Tempered	Reinforcing
Feverishly	Stifled	Quivering
Violently	Mandated	Feigned
Beckoned	Bravado	Gratitude
Indifferent	Regardless	Dosage
Scrutinize	Envision	Ceaselessly
Portent		

Chapter 12

Mundane	Plentiful	Awkwardly
Shrill	Spellbound	Downtrodden
Wary	Anguish	Embodiment
Captivating	Fathomed	Confident

Teacher's Classroom Guide: Before Reading

Learning Creatively

Class projects can help ensure that each student's reading of *Magic Lands: Journey Beyond the Beyond* is a unique experience that touches them personally. Class projects can also help students better understand, summarize, and review the book.

A few ideas for class projects include:

- **Reading Journals**   Ask students to create a journal for *Magic Lands: Journey Beyond the Beyond*. Don't grade the journal. Instead make it an activity that allows students to reflect without being corrected or worrying about a letter grade. Tell the students that the purpose of the journal is to record any thoughts, ideas, or questions they might have as they read *Magic Lands: Journey Beyond the Beyond*.

    If any students need help getting started, ask them to write one or more things they learned after reading each chapter, or ask them to write about a character or event that was in the chapter they just read. To show students that you are reviewing the journal, enter nonjudgmental comments or use stickers, such as smiley faces where they've done a good job expressing themselves.

- **Individual Projects**   Ask students to choose a scene from the book and illustrate it, or to create a drawing of a certain place in the story, such as the place lost and deep. Suggest that they reread the chapter containing the scene they want to use before they get started. If they want to illustrate several scenes, they could create a picture book to share with the class or others.

- **Partner Projects**   Select intriguing scenes or interesting paragraphs from *Magic Lands: Journey Beyond the Beyond*. You should have one scene or paragraph for every two students in the class. Pair each student with a partner and have them read the scene or paragraph. Ask the students to read and discuss the scene or paragraph with their partner, and then write in their own words what they think it means. Encourage students to think of different ways the scene or paragraph could be interpreted and to illustrate their work as well.

An Interview with Robert Stanek

Family and Childhood

How many brothers and sisters do you have?

I was the fourth child of five and the only boy. My oldest sister was a teenager when I was born. We lived in a small, green, two-story house in the city then. I remember she didn't like me going into her room. She could be mean sometimes if she thought I was bothering her.

But she wasn't really mean. I think I just pestered her a lot. When I started kindergarten, she would walk me to school to make sure I was okay. Big sisters are like that. They want their privacy and they don't really mean to hurt your feelings.

Did bullies ever pick on you?

My neighborhood was tough. My mom never wanted us to walk alone. We had a lot of bullies in our neighborhood.

If you weren't a fighter, you'd better be a runner. I was a scrawny kid so I learned how to run fast. The problem is you couldn't always run. I remember my bicycle was stolen one year while I was playing with friends. The bicycle had been a gift from my Big Brother and it meant the world to me.

Tell me about your Big Brother.

My siblings are all girls, so I never had a brother. Big Brothers Big Sisters is a volunteer, youth services organization. I was something of a whiz kid. I took the standardized tests in the fourth grade. I think that was the first time I'd ever been tested like that and the results that came back astonished everyone. It was a real "Malcolm-in-the-Middle" moment and you could say the character of Malcolm is a lot like I was at that age. The teachers wanted to advance me to the sixth grade but my mom wouldn't let them. She didn't want anyone to give me special treatment. Looking back, I think that was a good thing.

Anyway, it was during this time that my mom got me into the Big Brother program. My Big Brother was a doctor, a psychologist. He took a special interest in mentoring me and would visit on the weekend. We talked a lot, went on drives, and visited places I'd never seen. His visits were special because I didn't have a dad, at least not one that cared enough to visit. It really meant a lot to me to have him as a Big Brother. I've always wanted to tell him that.

Did you read a lot when you were a child?

You bet I did. We couldn't afford to buy books but that didn't stop me from reading. I remember going to the library with my mom. We'd go at least once a week and I could pick out any books I wanted. I thought I was the luckiest kid in the world. I didn't know or care that we were poor.

I remember being fascinated with the *Ripley's Believe It Or Not* books and *Guinness Book of World Records*. I loved the fantastic stories of people who could do incredible things, like swallowing swords or walking on fire.

I wasn't your typical young reader. I don't remember ever reading picture books. I do remember the librarians helping me find new books to read. They got me reading a lot of the classics—classics I still love like *Treasure Island*, *The Swiss Family Robinson*, *Kidnapped*, *Robinson Crusoe*, and *The Three Musketeers*.

I remember getting absolutely hooked on Jules Verne. I read *Around the World in Eighty Days*, *Twenty Thousand Leagues under the Sea*, and *Journey to the Center of the Earth*. I remember when *Journey to the Center of the Earth* came to the movies. I begged my mom for money so my little sister and I could go see it. We watched the movie three times that day. The only reason we left is because someone finally noticed these two kids who weren't leaving the theater when the movie ended. Back then they didn't really check the theaters like they do now.

I also went through a Sherlock Holmes phase. I read every Sir Arthur Conan Doyle book I could find in the library. Those books led me to Edgar Rice Burroughs, but I'm not quite sure why now. I do remember reading the Tarzan books over and over, and it was through Burroughs that I discovered science fiction. His *The Martian Tales* series got me hooked on the genre. I went on to read Ray Bradbury's *The Martian Chronicles* and liked it so much I read *The Illustrated Man*, *Something Wicked This Way Comes*, and *Fahrenheit 451*.

Teacher's Classroom Guide: An Interview with Robert Stanek

These are all books I read before my tenth birthday, so yes, I really did read a lot and I loved to read more than anything else.

Did you want to be a writer back then?

I'm not sure if I ever wanted to be a writer when I was younger. I did have a lot of influences leading me in that direction, though. I had a relative who worked for Golden Books in Racine. I think he used to give us kids activity and coloring books on birthdays and holidays.

In grade school I wrote for the school newspaper, and by the fourth grade I was a Junior Editor. I wrote several weekly columns, including the school sports column. I remember writing stories, but I think the earliest things I wrote were jokes and riddles. When I was five or six I thought they were funny, but looking back I don't think they were that funny.

I kept a journal back then and that's where I wrote down my stories and jokes. I would also paste my columns from the school newspaper in it.

I was always fascinated by the lives of the writers whose stories I read. I always wanted to know how they lived, what they did, what life was like when they were alive, why they wrote. I would look up their biographies in the *Encyclopedia Britannica*. I remember getting a card game one year for Christmas that had to do with famous authors. It showed pictures of the authors, listed a brief biography. I played that game a lot and studied the cards. To me, those cards were better than baseball cards.

Did you have any pets when you were little?

In the city, we had a dog named Lobo. He was a Siberian husky. He helped watch the house and keep us kids safe. He had two different colored eyes. He was a great dog. In the winter he would pull us around in a sled. Since he was such a big dog, he usually stayed outside. He had a big thick chain attached to a spike in the ground and I always felt sorry for him when it was cold out. The dog next door would always bark at him, and one day Lobo broke his chain, jumped the fence, and killed the dog. It was a Great Dane and the owner was so mad he made us put Lobo down. I was heartbroken for a long time.

I got a tomcat after that. He was a cute kitten and grew to be huge. I've never seen a cat that big since. He liked to sneak out and roam the neighborhood. He would get in fights and sometimes wouldn't come home for days. Before we moved to the country, he got out. We'd go back to the old house to check for him hoping he'd be there but he never was. I never saw him again after that.

And we had another dog, Toby, who was around until after I went to the military. We also had other cats. One of the cats lived over 20 years and my mother kept her after all us kids moved out.

Tell us about your father and mother.

My father was a Hungarian immigrant. He came to America after the Hungarian Uprising in 1956. He fought to keep the Communists out of Hungary and was sent to a Prisoner of War camp in Yugoslavia after Budapest fell to the Communists. He escaped from the Prisoner of War camp and made his way to America where he hoped to start over. Part of his story appeared in an issue of *Life* Magazine.

When he arrived in New York, he found work at the J. I. Case tractor factory. Some years later he worked construction and later started his own construction company. He was a hard worker, but also haunted by what he'd seen growing up in Hungary during World War II and fighting during the Hungarian Uprising. I think that's why he drank so heavily.

My mother was the granddaughter of Norwegian and French immigrants who came to America with their parents. She, like my father, was a hard worker, but the two were never happy together. After they divorced, my mother raised us five kids by herself. That was hard for her, and for us. To make ends meet, she was always working. She worked a minimum-wage day job, and cleaned houses in the evenings and often on weekends. She tried not to show how tired she was after coming home from 12 to 16 hour days, but she was always tired.

Whenever my mom lost a job, things got tough. My grandparents could only help out so much and my mom didn't want to go on welfare except as a last resort, which it sometimes was. I remember weeks at a time where we ate nothing but flour and water pancakes at home. If it weren't for school lunches, I don't know what we would have done; but I don't regret growing up poor, my childhood or anything.

I learned a lot of life lessons early: the value of hard work, the value of money, the value of close family. My mother always made sure it was a happy house. The holidays were big at our house. Thanksgiving, Christmas, New Years were all big to-do's even if the food and the gifts were donations from the Salvation Army.

Teacher's Classroom Guide: An Interview with Robert Stanek

Did you always do as you were told?

Everyone makes mistakes. I wasn't perfect. Growing up in a rough neighborhood, I wasn't what you'd call an angel. I had to be smarter and faster than the bullies. If I wasn't fast enough, I had to fight or give up my lunch money or whatever else they wanted.

One time, it was the family groceries I was carrying back from the corner store, and that hurt a lot because we didn't have money to replace what was stolen and I knew that. I started stealing things after that. I don't know why, but I imagine it had something to do with trying to get even for what had happened.

When I was visiting friends of my mom's I got caught shoplifting, but I still hadn't learned my lesson. Later that same day, I stole some money from them and got caught again. I wasn't a very good thief, and it's a good thing. It was pure agony, and then getting caught—not once but twice—I learned my lesson quick.

Needless to say, my mom's friends didn't want us kids at their house after that—and me in particular.

Tell us about your grandparents.

My grandparents were a huge influence on my life. After the stealing incidents, some parents might have wanted to ship me off to military school. I was only seven or eight at the time, and while I might have been threatened with it, my grandparents thought of a better solution. They started sending us kids to Christian Bible Camp.

I think I went for the first time the year I was caught stealing, so I thought it was supposed to be a punishment. You know, send that darn kid away to find God and maybe he'll notice one of the Ten Commandments has to do with stealing.

The camp was called Camp Timber Lee. It was located in the heart of Wisconsin's farm country. I remember that kids of different age groups went at different times. My little sister cried and cried at summer camp. She was homesick every day. She wanted to go home.

When it came my turn to go, I was petrified. I didn't know what to expect, but when I got there I found out they had all these activities you could do. You could learn about nature, go on hikes, make arts and crafts, take archery lessons, go swimming, go sailing. And, oh yeah, you couldn't skip certain things, like the bible lessons or the nighttime gatherings.

To my surprise, I loved camp and the best part about it was the nighttime gatherings where everyone got together to sing and learn about the bible. The next summer I hoped I could go again, but my grandparents paid for my cousins to go.

Fate was on my side though. My cousins hated camp, and as I was the only one who liked it, I got to go every summer after that.

The funny thing is that Camp Timber Lee really did change my outlook on life. I learned so much there. I learned how to swim, how to sail, how to kayak. I learned how to survive in nature. I also learned important lessons about values, morals, truth, and friendship. I made lifelong friends at camp. I even met my first girlfriend there.

My one regret about those summers is that I never did learn how to ride horses. Horseback riding was something that cost extra and I never did get up the courage to ask my grandparents if they'd pay for the lessons. It was enough that they were already paying for me to go to camp.

So now whenever I think of my grandparents, I think of Camp Timber Lee and all the things I learned and experienced there. Looking back, I'm sure going away from home every summer is what gave me the courage to leave home when it came time—and that was a good thing. It was the first, necessary step to becoming a best-selling writer.

Why did you move to the country?

My mom wanted us kids to have a normal life and she worked really hard to make sure we had as normal a life as we could. With my older sisters out of the house and just me and my little sister at home, she was afraid to leave us alone when she had to work at night or on the weekend. I could get into a lot of mischief in a few hours and so could my sister. Add to that the attempted burglary of our home—our dog Toby bit the gun-toting burglar on the butt—and I think my mom was more than ready to get out of the city.

The opportunity came when she found a farmhouse that hadn't been rented out in a while. The farmhouse was old, drafty, and required a lot of upkeep. But my mom didn't care about that. It was perfect, and she made sure it was perfect for us.

I still remember that yard. It was huge and had to be tended to—and we couldn't afford a fancy mower. We actually used a push mower—the kind powered by you pushing rather than an engine—to mow the lawn. I learned a lot about the value of hard work, following a schedule, and persistence helping to mow that lawn.

That lawn was something that had to be tended to every week or otherwise it was almost impossible to mow the next week. And it took hours and hours to finish, so we usually couldn't finish it all in a day. Instead, we spread out the mowing over several days.

Tell us about the farmhouse and growing up in the country.

The house was an old two-story farmhouse on several acres of land. The long gravel drive that ran for several hundred yards from the road is the first thing I remember seeing. After that I remember going out into the yard. The yard had an apple tree, a cherry tree, a few oak trees, a big hill, and a sunken area that as a kid I imagined was a valley.

The house was just at the start of a small lakeside community and we were within walking distance of the lake. In the summer, my sister and I would spend all day walking around the lake, chasing frogs and fish. There was a store on one side of the lake where we'd go buy soda pop and snacks if we found some change.

In the other direction, there were farm fields. A stream ran through the fields and we'd follow it endlessly when the weather was warm. We'd pretend to be adventurers. If you followed the stream for a few miles, there was a dump that had been used by farmers a long time ago.

We found a lot of cool stuff there. Mostly old beer cans and bottles, but the stuff was fifty years old so we thought it was treasure. If you walked another few miles, you ended up in a small town, and we sometimes stopped in the general store there; or we'd go over by the mushroom farm and watch the horses run in the fields.

In the fall we'd build giant leaf piles and jump into them. One time I burrowed into the hill under the leaf pile, thinking I was something of a hobbit. It was the same time that the badgers moved into the brush down the hill—so digging a huge, inviting hole wasn't a good idea as I later found out.

In the winter, we'd build these huge snow forts. We'd add to the snow fort as long as the snow and cold weather lasted. Sometimes we'd end up with a dozen tunnels and rooms, all under the snow.

What else do you remember about living there?

Well, living in the country wasn't all peaches and cream. We had neighborhood bullies there too. One in particular picked on my sister and me every day, at least until I decided I had had enough. He tried to pick on me in the schoolyard and I got up just enough courage to stand up to him. I think he won the fight, because I ended up with him sitting on me, pummeling me, but he got the black eye and never bothered me again after that.

I remember also that the bus rides from school were incredibly long. On the way to school, we were the last to be picked up, so we went straight to school, but on the way home we were the last to get off the bus. We went out deep into farm country before going back to where I lived and that took over an hour, sometimes an hour and a half.

Long bus rides like that were boring. I read a lot to pass the time.

What was it like not having your father in your life?

Not having a father in my life was painful. It was lonely sometimes. He rarely called or visited. It was as though us kids just weren't a part of his life that was important. To make things worse, he never paid child support.

The only time he ever sent us anything or bought us anything was at Christmas. When I was older he'd sometimes send a few hundred dollars through Western Union. That was it, and let me tell you a few hundred dollars didn't go far.

I have few memories of visiting my father when he lived in Wisconsin with his second wife. The first time I clearly remember visiting him is when I was ten or twelve. My mom, my younger sister, and I took a trip to Mississippi, where he lived at that time. It was a fun trip. He bought us clothes, took us out fishing on his boat. We went out to eat a lot and I remember a big barbeque.

That trip was one of the happiest and one of the saddest times of my life. I was happy because the Gulf Coast is a beautiful place to visit and because I was with my father. I was sad because it was the first time that I realized my father was wealthy. He was running a construction business in Mississippi and Texas. He had three houses, a 40' boat, cars, trucks, all kinds of expensive things. On the other side of that was my mom and us kids struggling to make ends meet, struggling just to get by.

I wondered if he'd care that I spent my free time mowing lawns and doing odd jobs just to help make ends meet. Somehow I didn't think he would, and that made me very sad.

After that trip, I'd visit sometimes in the summer. I remember visiting when I was fifteen or sixteen, then again when I was seventeen.

School Days

Tell me about your first school.

My first school was Janes School Elementary in Racine, Wisconsin. Janes School is in a turn-of-the-century schoolhouse.

The main section was built in the late 1800s and is the same school that my grandfather attended for several years during his primary school days. In the early 1900s there were two schools running out of the same building: one on the first floor and another on the second floor. My grandfather went to the school on the second floor.

I loved that old school. It had oak floors and the lower level was split into several sections. You went down one set of stairs to go to the gym and cafeteria, then after lunch we'd go up a different set of stairs to go out into the schoolyard.

As a kindergartner, I remember being afraid of all those stairs but they were fun once I learned how to navigate them.

My first teacher was very strict. It was a public school, but she had a lot of rules of her own that were probably carried over from her days in private schools.

One of those rules was that children shouldn't write with their left hand. Bad children wrote with their left hand. Good children wrote with their right hand. At least that's how it was in her day and in her mind.

I remember getting whacked on the knuckles every time I tried to color or draw with my left hand. I came home with a swollen hand one day and couldn't move my fingers. My mom walked me right back to school and had it out with the teacher. The teacher never whacked me with a ruler again. I'm still left-handed by the way.

Tell me about your walks to school.

I really loved walking to school. I remember the whole walk—it was about four blocks—but it seemed like miles back then. Everything seems so big or long when you're small. We lived in a tough neighborhood so I didn't walk alone much, but sometimes I did and I was really scared.

A few years ago I went back to Racine and visited the neighborhood where I grew up. The green, two-story house was still there. It looked exactly like it did when I lived there. I also drove along the route I used to take to school. I couldn't believe it was only a few blocks—I still had this memory of how long the walk was and how far away the school was.

I was delighted to find that the old school was still there too. I went in and visited, surprised at all the memories that the visit brought back. Despite the ruler-whacking incident, I really loved that school. All my teachers after kindergarten were wonderful and I attended Janes School until the fourth grade. After that, we moved to the country and I attended Wheaton Elementary.

What do you remember about that school?

Wheaton Elementary was different than I expected. In the city, the next year I would have been in fifth grade and been one of the big kids in the schoolyard, and being big or small made a huge difference as you know from my comments about bullies. I was also the older brother taking my younger sister to school, so I felt like I had a tremendous amount of responsibility.

When we moved, I found out the new school went from Kindergarten to eighth grade and instead of walking we rode the school bus. So not only was I not one of the big kids any more, I also didn't have any big brother responsibilities. I had looked forward to being the big brother for a change.

I soon found out that was the least of my worries. I had no friends at the new school. I didn't know anyone and it was my bad luck to get seated within spitting distance from the class bully. I went from being one of the happiest, most attentive kids to being one of the most miserable.

I hated school for a while after that. I went from being very outgoing to being someone who rarely said anything. I didn't want to go to school sometimes. I'd beg to stay home. My mom would let me sometimes.

I hid in my books for a long time. But it wasn't all bad. The school had a great library. It was easily twice the size as the library at my old school.

That year I discovered Herman Melville, Jack London, Charles Dickens, and Edgar Allan Poe. Edgar Allan Poe can be pretty bleak and dark, especially when you're ten years old. But I remember being fascinated with his stories. To this day, I can still remember parts of *The Raven*, *The Tell Tale Heart*, and *The Murders in the Rue Morgue*.

Those books and stories became like friends, so it made things a lot better. I did eventually make friends and I started liking school again, so that made things better too.

Tell us about moving and changing schools.

I've probably moved more than anyone you'll ever know. Being in the military, I had to move around a lot with my own family as well. My son asked me one time how many times I moved in my life. I stopped to think about it and it took about ten minutes to figure out. I counted eighteen moves—seven of those when I was a kid. Personally, I think there's some Hungarian gypsy blood in me, but can't confirm it.

Back to that move, that time we moved closer to the city because my mom got a new job in the sheriff's department. The timing was awful. We moved partway through my freshman year of high school (ninth grade).

High School was different from grade school. In our area kids for all over the county attended one of two high schools, so kids from many different grade schools attended each. It was a big adjustment for me because the school was terrifyingly huge. Then just when I made a bunch of new friends and learned how to get around the school, we moved.

I went from Wilmot High School to Central High School. Because the schools zones weren't that far apart, some of the kids from my old school went there, but none of them were my friends. Basically, I had to start all over: make new friends, learn how to get around the school, all of it.

Moving a lot as a child was really awful and it was lonely a lot of the time, but I met a lot more people and was exposed to much more than the average kid. I learned a lot about people and myself because of all those moves. I had a lot of great teachers along the way.

In the end, I think all those moves better prepared me for life. I know people that are scared to death of moving. They don't want to leave the area they grew up. They don't want things to change. They want everything just as it was.

The problem with that is that things do change. You have to adapt and move on. If you don't you may get stuck living in the past where the best time of your life is your school days and not the present where you should be happy and fulfilled.

My younger sister is a perfect example of that. I think all those moves made her more resistant to change. After graduation she stayed in the same small town for the next 20 years, worked minimum wage jobs, barely got by.

A few years ago she and her husband decided to make a positive change in their life. Their church was a big influence in the decision and I'm thankful for that.

They moved with their family to a place where they could both make a living wage and had opportunities to grow their skills. So far so good, they now enjoy a comfortable life and have money to take vacations and travel.

Who was your favorite teacher?

With all those moves and new schools, I had many favorite teachers. The teachers I remember clearest in my memory are my high school teachers. I was always a strong student, even when I was a bit rebellious, so I was in the advanced and honors classes. You know, honors English all that.

In the sciences, I took biology, chemistry and physics. My biology/physics teacher was a lot of fun. He was a bit portly and had a beard. He would tell jokes and do silly things that just made learning fun. Our school was one of the first to get computers—remember, I went to high school in the 1980s and computers were just starting to be available for home and school use.

We had Apple IIs and the same teacher was in that class too. It was on the honor system, so you just went to the computer lab and did whatever as long as you turned in the assignments.

Computers opened up a whole new world for me. By the end of the year, I was programming game code in binary and assembly. I made a game called *Beer Wars* where you had to blast pretzels, beer kegs, and beer bottles—you can probably tell I was going through a bit of a rebellious stage then.

With computers, I was hooked right from the start.

Another teacher that was a big influence on me was my mathematics teacher. I advanced in math through calculus in high school. My calculus teacher was a brilliant man. Problem is I had his class first thing in the morning. At that time, I was running with the wrong crowd of kids, doing things at all hours of the night that I shouldn't have been doing.

I would always get to his class late. I'd have to stop off in the bathroom too because I had these wicked allergies. I never had allergies before so I didn't know what to do. My nose was always running. If I were going to school today, the teachers probably would've thought I was on drugs but I wasn't into those types of things.

Drugs are bad for you. They'll mess you up for life. I knew better than to use drugs. One of my sisters had smoked marijuana and I remember what happened when my mom found out.

I didn't know about alcohol though. My father was an alcoholic, so I thought drinking was okay. Even at a young age, I remember visiting my father sometimes and stealing beer when he wasn't watching. I'd run off with his wife's kids from his second marriage and go drink it. So when I got older, I thought it was okay to drink too. But drinking can be as bad as drugs. It was screwing up my life.

Anyway this teacher was a big help. I think he knew I was screwing up and may have suspected what I was doing. He didn't punish me or turn me in though. I had an A+ average in his class, never missed a point, so I think that was part of it. It was the one time in my life I ever got special treatment for being smart and it helped.

Another teacher that was a big influence on me was my typing teacher, believe it or not. She was the greatest. At that time, we worked on a mix of electric and manual typewriters. I was one of the only boys in a class full of girls. The only boy in Typing II, when I took a second semester, that's for sure.

People thought this honors student was taking typing to goof off. But that wasn't it at all. When I started programming computers, I recognized immediately how important being able to type was to programming and if there was ever a better typing teacher, I've never met one.

By the end of that second semester, I was typing sixty words per minute. We learned business skills in those classes too. Those skills have helped me in every job I've ever held. And I don't think I'd be a writer if I didn't know how to type. I'd be too frustrated.

Was there anything you didn't like about school?

Well that's a funny question. Isn't it?

I didn't always like school. I did have some teachers that were mean. I remember clearly

Teacher's Classroom Guide: An Interview with Robert Stanek

an English teacher who gave me an F on a test that was one-third of the grade, which gave me a D+ for the semester. She said I didn't follow directions, but I did. She was a bully of the worst sort and it's easy for teachers to use their authority to be bullies.

I don't think she liked this poor kid with ragged clothes in her honors class. Our house had burned down that year, so I was wearing hand-me-downs from the Salvation Army and Goodwill. I didn't fit in with the other kids and their middle class backgrounds.

That teacher should have been the one to help me the most because she was in a position to. She helped other kids. Instead of helping me, she made sure my grade point average didn't threaten any of her stars.

People who think being smart is a ticket to success don't understand life. There are a lot of smart people who never get a chance.

That incident taught me one of the great truths of my life. I already knew other kids disliked brainiac/nerd types, but that was my first experience with an adult, someone I looked up to. It was like a wake up call to force myself to be genuinely average, to coast by, to not stand out, to not get noticed. That's how much of an impact that incident had on my life.

Staggering success as an underachiever is overrated though. You get nowhere, become nothing. All through my school days I would've traded brains for brawn any time. The jocks, the school athletes, were the ones teachers rewarded and all the kids liked.

But what I discovered much later in life changed my viewpoint on that. What I discovered is that some people will feel threatened if you are smart. Some people will dislike you because you are smart. They might not hire you. They might not promote you. They might try to discredit you. You may get a new boss of this type who may fire you or make you so miserable you quit.

I've found this to be true in the military, in Fortune 500 companies, in small business. It's sad but it's true everywhere. I've found few exceptions.

Truth is though, if you work hard and are willing to stand up for yourself, you can make it. You can achieve your dreams.

Never give up.

When you make it, do me a favor. Look back fondly on your past. Forget about all those people who tried to hold you back, who put you down, who made you feel unimportant.

Remember instead the ones who helped. Remember instead that adversity made you stronger, better. Remember that there are people who understand what you're going through, what you went through. The world isn't a perfect place, but for each and every one of us, it is what we decide to make it.

Outside of school, what was your childhood like?

I don't think there are a lot of people who have a childhood like mine. I knew at a young age that my life was anything but charmed. There was a lot of tragedy in my life. That tragedy shaped who I was then and who I am today.

When I was very young my mom remarried. He was a former navy enlisted man. They were truly in love. They bought a house in Sturtevant, Wisconsin. Shortly afterward, my younger sister was born. It was a very happy time, but all too short, like most such times in my life.

One day, my stepdad went to down to the basement to check the gas hot water heater because we had no hot water. A repairman had been out to fix the hot water heater several times, but it never worked right. When my stepdad struck a match to relight the heater, the whole house exploded. The heater had been leaking gas and it was everywhere.

He was engulfed in flames and was burned over 80 percent of his body. My sister, Bridgette, who had been standing behind him, was knocked out the basement door by the blast.

She was rushed to the hospital with my stepdad. The hospital was very busy that day. My stepdad was rushed away to a burn unit, where he died a few days later.

All us kids waited in the emergency room with my mom. My mom kept asking the nurse to look at my sister, but no one ever did. A few hours later, Bridgette just closed her eyes and never woke up again. She had a brain injury—something doctors and nurses now know to look for after that type of trauma, but I don't think they did back then.

I remember crying for days. It was a sad time. It was right after that that we moved to the green two-story house in Racine.

Have you ever gone back to the schools you attended?

I did actually. Being in the military kept me away from Wisconsin for a long time, and it was twenty years before I made an extended visit and had time to travel around a bit.

I visited Janes School Elementary first, surprised at how many memories that brought back. I hadn't been in the old schoolhouse for all those years, but I remembered it. I remembered my first grade classroom, the halls, all those stairs that made the school seem like a labyrinth. I remembered the cafeteria and the gym, and the schoolyard where I pitched marbles.

Visiting my other schools brought a flood of memories too.

Did you really get leeches all over you one time?

I did. When we moved to the farmhouse, there was that stream nearby. We'd go there and play all the time. The stream bed was real muddy, and a lot of time as we followed the stream we'd slosh in the water. Sometimes in our bare feet, sometimes with our tennis shoes on.

We knew the stream had leeches because most of the time if you stepped too deep in the mud you'd take your foot out and find leeches. *Eek*!

You could pinch them and pull them off. If you were fast, they wouldn't have a chance to get a good hold of your flesh, but a lot of the time you had to rip them off and that hurt.

One time, I was trying to cross the stream, walking on top of a row of rocks. The rocks were slippery and wet from my sister sloshing across just before me. I never made it across. I fell on my backside into the water. With the water running fast from the spring runoff, it took my some time to get out. I got stuck in the muck on the far bank too.

I felt them crawling on me right away. By the time I ripped my shirt off, I knew they were everywhere. I had to take off my shoes, my socks, my pants.

My sister helped me start pulling all the leeches off. They were on my back, legs, between my toes, under my arms. I was just happy they didn't manage to get someplace else, though. You know where.

Oh! that would have been painful. It's painful even thinking about it now.

Did you watch a lot of television?

Well, we didn't have cable TV back then, so there really wasn't much to watch. I know some parts of the city did. I remember my grandpa had cable. We didn't. We used a rabbit ears antenna on top of the TV.

We were lucky to be close to Chicago and Milwaukee though, so we got some channels. I remember watching WGN out of Chicago the most. It played a lot of oldies and I liked the black and white shows the best.

I'd watch *The Three Stooges, Gilligan's Island, Mr. Ed, Superman*. I remember getting up at 5 a.m. to watch *Topper* and *The Lone Ranger*. I liked the old *Abbott and Costello* movies, too.

On the weekend, they had *Creature Theater*. I'd watch *Dracula, Frankenstein, Godzilla, The Mummy*, that kind of stuff. But I really didn't watch that much TV.

Instead of watching TV, I read or listened to old radio programming. I had a whole collection of oldies on tape. *The Green Hornet, War of the Worlds, The Lone Ranger* again—I liked stories with clear heroes and villains.

Do you miss those times?

For me it really was the best of times and the worst of times. I do miss it sometimes.

It wasn't all sugar and gumdrops, but it's what I had. Like I said, my mom always worked hard to make sure we had as happy a home as possible. That was huge for me.

Every kid needs one person who loves them that much. A dad, a mom, a brother, a sister, an uncle, an aunt, a teacher, whatever. It really does make all the difference. If you don't have that kind of support, there are places to find it. The Boy Scouts and Girls Scouts of America, Big Brothers Big Sisters, the YMCA to name a few.

My mom knew she couldn't do it all. She sowed the seeds, got us interested in things: museums, libraries, Boy Scouts, Girl Scouts, church. Then she let us decide what we wanted to do.

One year, you know, the one where I was caught stealing, she started sending us kids to Sunday school. Between Christian Bible Camp in the summer and Christian Bible School on Sundays, I got the message and mended my ways pretty darn quick.

After that, Sunday school became optional. Go if you want to.

My sister and I did go for a few more years.

A car hit you when you were young. What happened?

Sometimes I feel like my childhood was a car wreck, but that one happened when I was in the fifth grade. It was the year after we moved to the farmhouse. I went out for a ride on a new bike. A gift from my Big Brother to replace the bike that had been stolen in the city.

I rode down the hill from our house, went around the corner. I remember looking down a stretch of straight road and then *wham!* the car hit me from behind. The driver was going really fast and the car slammed into the bike like it wasn't there. The bike ended up with the back tire twisted around all the way to where the front tire used to be, before it broke off the frame. I flew off the bike and landed on the pavement. The car drove over the bike and stopped just after it drove over me and started to drag me down the road.

The driver was a drunken school teacher. She picked me up off the road, put my bike in the trunk of her car, and then drove to her house. I was unconscious so I don't remember exactly, but I know she never called for an ambulance.

She called her husband, waited till she sobered up. It must have taken a few hours because by the time my mom came and got me it was dark out, and I had gone out for the ride early in the afternoon.

I was conscious then, barely, scraped and bruised from head to toe. My clothes were all torn up, shredded like I'd been dragged behind the car. But I didn't have any broken bones.

The school teacher told my mom she'd hit me with her car and I'd scraped my knee, could she come and get me. I remember my mom screaming and screaming when she saw me. It was the school teacher's husband or her son who carried me out to my mom's car. Afterward, I remember he put my broken up bike in the back of my mom's station wagon and then they pretty much closed the door in my mom's face.

I missed a few weeks of school, recovering in a chair next to the TV. It was a miserable time because I hurt everywhere and the pain was intense whenever I moved. We couldn't afford a hospital, so I stayed in that chair till I got better. I don't remember ever visiting a doctor either.

The school teacher never checked to see how I was doing. An insurance adjuster showed up a few weeks later. He convinced my mom that $500 and a new bike was worth signing a paper saying that we weren't going to sue.

Military Career

Why did you join the military?

That's the $64,000 question, isn't it? I've been asked that a lot. Smart kid should have gotten a scholarship, gone to a good school. But that's not how it worked out.

I didn't know how to apply for scholarships, loans, or grants. I had no idea where to begin. There was no one there to help. No one in my family had ever gone to college so no one knew how that stuff worked. My mom was always working.

At school, teachers that maybe should have helped focused on other kids—you know the ones with parents who could afford to pay for college, or most of it—and the school programs were all about preparing for the SAT or taking the AFQT (Armed Forces Qualifying Test). They didn't teach us anything about what we needed to do to get into college.

I took the SAT because it got me out of school for a day. My scores were respectable for someone who never prepared for the exam or cared about the score. I would have had my choice of several colleges if I had applied. But who was going to pay for it?

I took the AFQT because they gave it in school—during school. My high score meant about as much as my SAT score—nothing, at least to me. Recruiters loved it though, and I had a sister that was already in the Air Force, so the Air Force recruiter was particularly persistent.

As my high school graduation day approached, I had no idea what I was going to do with my life. To complicate matters, my mom had just remarried. She moved with her new husband and my sister to northern Wisconsin a few months before graduation. I stayed with a friend so I could finish out the school year and go to graduation.

After graduation I visited my dad in Mississippi. I had worked for him before in the summer, doing roofing and siding. It paid well but the hours were long. Most of the summer we'd work sunup till sundown, and let me tell you, there are few places hotter than the side of a building or a roof in the summer.

I already knew construction was something I didn't want to do for a living, but I went anyway. It gave me a destination, a place to go.

I mentioned to my dad that I wanted to go to college. He got me interested in an aeronautical engineering school in Florida. He had been a pilot in the Hungarian Air Force. We visited the school, but I knew right away that my father had no intention of paying for it.

Instead, he wanted me to join the Air Force so I could fly planes like he did. The only problem was that he didn't understand that I'd never be a pilot without a college degree. He didn't need a degree to fly, so why would I? But that's the way it is in the U.S. military.

We visited the Air Force recruiter that same week. I took the ASVAB (Armed Services Vocational Aptitude and Battery Test) a few days later. With my scores, the recruiter told me I could enlist and get any specialty I wanted. He even told my dad that I could become an aircraft mechanic and get stationed right there in Mississippi.

My dad loved that idea. I didn't so much, so after the summer I went back to Wisconsin. My mom was living in northern Wisconsin, so that's where I went.

By the holidays I was completely miserable. I didn't know many people. I didn't have a job. I knew my life was going nowhere. I knew I needed to make a change or I'd be stuck going down a one-way street into a dead end.

I decided to go talk to the Air Force recruiter again. We talked a lot about the career fields that were available and where I'd fit in with my skills. The career field that got my interest was Intelligence, and the particular specialty of cryptologic linguist.

All the training associated with that career fascinated me. Weeks of intensive language school, weeks of analytics school, weeks of specialty training. Nearly two years of training in all. I thought it'd be like getting a degree only better—I'd have a sure job waiting at the end of it all.

I enlisted right then.

What do you remember about basic training?

The Air Force conducts basic training at Lackland Air Force Base in San Antonio, Texas. I flew from Milwaukee to New Orleans, and then the next day I took a military bus to San

Antonio. That bus ride was the longest of my life. I knew basic training was at the end of it and I'll be the first to admit I was scared.

Someone should have told me from the start that basic training was a head game designed to break you down and rebuild you as a model soldier. As a thinker, I would have understood it a lot better. I got by, though.

The drill sergeants start by taking away your identity. They strip you of all your belongings—your ties to home and family. They shave men's hair, cut women's hair, then put everyone in a uniform. Every trainee should look like every other trainee. That's the thinking.

I was an ugly bald guy.

Drill teaches discipline. Classroom instruction teaches military rules and codes of conduct.

All the other stuff—ironing your clothes, polishing your boots, folding your bed sheets—is pretty much designed to teach conformity and uniformity. It also keeps your thoughts focused on basic training and helps you to forget about your life outside the military.

It worked pretty well too. I was frequently terrified. I graduated basic training with honors, a model soldier.

Was language school hard?

The first day of language school was a wake up call for me. I thought that since basic training was over life would go back to normal. That was hardly the case.

At that time, the Air Force trained linguists at Lackland Air Force Base and at Presidio of Monterrey, California. I thought I'd be going to California. I was ready to learn how to surf. Instead of going to California, though, I stayed in Texas—it seemed to be the start of forty-seven weeks of hell.

Language school at Lackland followed many of the same rules as basic training. We had daily inspections, drill, physical training (PT), marching—the whole enchilada. It really felt like an extended basic training. To make matters worse, my training instructor singled me out as the one he was going to wash out, i.e. force out of the program.

He tried for forty-seven weeks to fail me out of the training program. He'd fail my room on inspections—even if it was spotless. We had 35-10 (military uniform and appearance) inspection once a week, so I knew when it was coming. I'd get a hair cut the day before but he'd still fail me and make me go get another hair cut.

Sometimes he'd give surprise inspections and fail me for not shaving. But I shaved every day. In basic training I had to shave twice a day to keep up the appearance of a baby smooth face. That tears up your face after a while though, so I couldn't shave twice a day every day.

While failing inspections gave me extra duties and kept me from getting liberties a lot of the time, it didn't fail me out of the training program. To get thrown out of the program, I would have also had to be failing my classes.

No, the only thing his bullying did was to keep my stress level high. I think he wanted me to quit because you could voluntarily quit the program and they'd send you to perform other duties—the types of duties the Air Force couldn't normally fill. One of my friends quit the program and the Air Force sent him to clean snow off runways in Alaska for the rest of his enlistment.

In fact, the fear of getting sent to that kind of duty is what kept many of us going. I had enlisted for four years and on the first day of language training our unit commander invited all sixty-five of us new trainees to look around the room. I'll never forget what he said. He said don't count on the person standing next to you being there in forty-seven weeks. He said don't count on anyone getting you through this training but you. He said ten of us wouldn't be here in two weeks, and most of the rest of us would be gone before graduation.

He was right. Only twenty-two out of sixty-five made it to graduation. The kicker was that language training was only the beginning. Each graduate had months of additional training to look forward to.

Where did you go next?

I went to Goodfellow Air Force Base, Texas. I spent the next twenty weeks learning how to be an analyst. When people think of intelligence analysts they often think of Tom Clancy's Jack Ryan. Jack Ryan's a fictitious character. What we were training to do was real.

We trained in a vault-like building with high security everywhere. There were guards, wire fences, dogs, security systems. We had to have top security clearances and badges to get into the building.

Analyst training was intense. Unlike language training we relied on each other a lot more to get through the days and weeks.

Teacher's Classroom Guide: An Interview with Robert Stanek

The training gave new meaning to the word stress. They worked us in rotating shifts to see if we could handle the rigor of changing schedules in addition to learning the job we would do in the field. Some people cracked under that pressure. They left the program because their grades slumped and they couldn't get back on track or because they simply were too tired of trying to make it through.

But for the most part, they didn't wash out because the instructors wanted them out. The instructors knew the value of training we'd already received. They'd move failing students back to a class that was just starting, give them a chance to start over, that kind of thing, if possible. Still, only fifteen of the twenty-two from my original group graduated and went on to field duties.

Did you like living in Texas?

Despite the fact that the early days in language training were like basic training, it wasn't all that way. Eventually, I did get into what was called Phase 3, which allowed me to go off base after hours and on weekends.

I had an old black Thunderbird, so I would cruise around San Antonio. When you are in such an intense environment, you make a lot of close friends. A group of us would go out on the town a lot. We'd go to the college bars uptown, the River Walk area, that kind of thing.

The Alamo is in San Antonio, so that was a fun visit. But the best time I ever had was tubing down the Guadeloupe River. Several classes of students went to the river that day. We rented these huge inner tubes and floated down the river all day.

Goodfellow is in San Angelo, Texas. It's a college town, so it had a great night scene and there was a lot to do on the weekends. Groups of us would go to a bar called O'Malley's. They had all you can eat specials several days a week. We spent a lot of time—and money—there.

The military had a great recreation area nearby with a lake. We'd rent boats, jet skis. Blow off a lot of steam.

Tell me about your first assignment.

Toward the end of training at Goodfellow AFB we had the chance to choose the bases we wanted to get stationed at. My top choice was Berlin, Germany. I wanted to be stationed right in the heart of East Germany. I wanted to see the Berlin Wall, plus I had heard that the base was in an old bunker complex. My second choice was Japan. I didn't know much about Japan at that time. I had heard it was beautiful and that there was a lot to see. My third choice was England. Being stationed in England would have been great.

The assignment I got was Japan. I'd be stationed at Misawa Air Base, Japan, attached to the Electronic Security Group. Five of the fifteen in my group went to Japan, in fact, but only one of those was someone I hung around with, so I was kind of sad. Then when we got to Japan, we all got assigned to different flights. There were Alpha, Bravo, Charlie, and Delta flights, plus a flight of day crew.

I was assigned to Charlie flight. It was late fall when I arrived in Japan, and over eighteen months since I had joined the air force. The building we worked in was a huge complex next to an enormous array of communications towers and a massive antennae structure called the Elephant Cage.

The facility was unique in that all branches of the U.S. armed forces worked there. We had army, air force, navy, and marines.

My first day on duty was a mid shift, meaning I had to work from midnight to 8 a.m. Let me tell you, it wasn't a good way to start.

We worked this crazy 4-4-4-3 rotation, which meant we worked four days (8 a.m. to 4 p.m.) had 24 hours off, then worked four swings (4 p.m. to 12 a.m.), followed by 24 hours off and four mids (12 a.m. to 8 a.m.). At the end of the rotation, we got 72 hours off.

Supposedly, this was a good shift rotation to work. I didn't buy it. But it was better than what our navy counterparts were working. They worked what was called double-backs. They worked two 8-hour day shifts followed by a 16-hour day-swing shift, followed by two swing shifts, a 16-hour swing-mid shift, and two mid shifts, before getting 96 hours off duty.

Anyway, that's how I remember my new supervisor breaking the news to me, that we basically worked twelve days and then got three off. Her "It could be worse" explanation worked pretty well. In fact, any time I felt worn out by the schedule, I remembered that and was thankful I didn't work the grinding ten-day crammed into eight days rotation that the navy worked.

Did training end once you got to your first assignment?

No. Right after my supervisor explained the rotating shift I'd be working she set down this huge pile of binders next to me. Then she began explaining that I had twelve weeks to learn everything that the binders contained. At that point, I remembered thinking "Or what?" What were they going to do to me if I just didn't want to learn any more? Wasn't all that training I had had supposed to prepare me for my first assignment?

Turned out that all the training was just leading up to the first assignment, providing the foundation as it were. In the field, each station had its own training regimen that was specific to the duties at that station, and the set of binders in front of me was just for one area of specialty. If I wanted to go into other specialty areas, I'd have to go through training for those specialties too.

She set a challenge before me, though. I felt compelled to accept. I loved being an Intelligence Analyst. She knew it too, from my prior training and grades. From the first day, we both knew I was a natural and by the second day, I was already working alone—something that took most new personnel several weeks.

I learned the material in four weeks, took and passed the exams with one of the highest scores they'd ever scene. I went into another specialty that would move me from direct operations to more intense field analysis. That training was supposed to last twelve weeks too, but I finished it in three.

By Christmas this fresh-from-training airman (me), was running the line analysis. I was telling Staff Sergeants and up what to do and when to do it. Let me tell you, that didn't go over too well and ruffled a few feathers.

But that's how it was. There was a chain of command and a rank structure, but if you were the best at the job, you determined what happened when and how things were done. It was a good thing that I had learned from past mistakes and knew better than to let it go to my head. I knew I walked a fine line. I didn't abuse the privilege.

Still, I lived and breathed that stuff. I received three more certifications, including one that was reserved only for the most advanced experts at that assignment. I liked the duty so much that at the end of the second year, I extended for another year.

Did you travel in Japan?

Japan is a wonderful, beautiful country. Back then I belonged to the school of work hard, play hard. I was in the Orient, the Far East. I wasn't about to let that opportunity pass me by.

Japan is an island nation with four large islands and many small islands. Honshû is the largest island and I was stationed in northern Honshû in the Tôhoku region. The area to the north of us was mountainous. I loved being able to visit the mountains and the ocean all in the same day.

On break I spent more time off base than on base. I traveled all over. On the Japanese island of Hokkaidô in Sapporo they have these wonderful Ice Festivals. The ice sculptures are amazing. I've never seen anything like it since.

In the spring, the Japanese celebrate the Cherry Blossom Festival. I'd go every year to a city in the northeast where they had these ancient temples and you could go walk around the grounds during the festival.

I'd take day trips to Aomori all the time. I liked that city. There was a lot to see and do and it was far enough away from the base that the people were very open and friendly.

My favorite trips were to Tokyo. Tokyo is in the Kantô region of Honshû so I could drive there. The road tolls were high though. Round trip it cost a few hundred dollars to drive and it was expensive to stay there, so I only went a few times, but I had a blast when I was there.

Did you learn Japanese?

I took Japanese classes and studied on my own as well. Spending a lot of time off base helped too. I had several friends who were Japanese. They'd help me with Japanese and I'd help them with English.

I was particularly smitten with a Japanese girl for a while, so that made me want to learn Japanese in a hurry so we could communicate. She was my first true love, but her family didn't want her to get so deeply involved with an American. We dated for a while and she came to see me when I left Japan, but we both knew it could be nothing more than it was.

Did you study martial arts?

I took kendo lessons, the Japanese art of fencing. I had the privilege of studying in one of the local martial arts training schools. At first, they weren't going to admit me. There weren't any other Americans training at the school, but I persisted.

I attended the sessions, watched the students training, learned as much as I could from watching. Finally, one day, the master presented me with my own kendo sword.

In Japan, martial arts are so much a part of the culture—like hotdogs, baseball, and apple pie are in the U.S. Japanese don't just take martial arts lessons. Martial arts are a part of who they are.

For many Japanese, it's not a question of whether they are going to learn martial arts, but what disciplines they are going to master. At least that's how it was explained to me, and for me it was a great honor and a privilege to be able to take lessons.

At my skill level though, I couldn't train with the adults. I had to train with the children. It was tough getting beaten by nine to ten year olds who had already been practicing kendo for many years. Most students start training at four or five. I learned humility in a hurry.

When I left Japan, I regretted that I hadn't started lessons earlier.

Where did you go after Japan?

In Japan I learned a lot about myself and what I could do as an Intelligence Analyst. One of my supervisors told me that I'd be a perfect candidate for airborne duty. Flying on secretive missions seemed extraordinarily appealing. I didn't give much thought to the fact that I could die doing that type of duty. Before my next assignment, I volunteered and was accepted into the airborne training program.

The first step in airborne training was survival school. After that I went to air combat school, then to a new assignment in Germany as a member of the combat crew flying on electronic warfare aircraft.

Was survival school really scary?

Survival school was one of the most exhilarating and challenging experiences of my life up until that time—and yes, it was a truly frightening experience at times. Training began with classroom instruction, then I went on to wilderness survival, prisoner of war training, and water survival training.

Survival school for the Air Force is conducted at Fairchild AFB, Washington. It was February when I went and bone cold in the mountains. I learned how to survive in the wilderness with nothing but the clothes on my back and a parachute. The same gear I'd have if a plane crash-landed somewhere and I had to parachute out of the plane.

I learned a lot: how to find food, what types of plants are edible, how to light a fire with flint and steal, how to get drinking water, how to find my way through the wilderness. That type of stuff.

The day after wilderness training, just when I would have had enough time to get a hot meal for the first time in weeks, they sent us on a bus ride. During that bus ride, "commandos" stormed the bus and took the entire team hostage. It seemed frightfully real at the time.

A black bag was put over my head, my hands were tied, and I was taken away with everyone else. The next thing I knew I was marching through a building and was then shoved into a tiny holding cell. I was alone in the dark.

The time was made worse by the music pouring out of the speakers. I'll never forget it. "Boot, boots, marching over Africa," the song went, and they played it over and over along with air raid sirens.

They kept me standing all through the night, hosed me down with cold water if I sat or fell asleep. The next morning they gave me dried oats and water. It was the only food served that day, and I had nothing the previous night.

I didn't eat and besides, before I could start, I was hauled away for "interrogation." The interrogators job was to break you down get you to say things. If you refused, you ended up in a box. I ended up in the box. The only way I could fit was to get into the fetal position. The box was dark and locked.

While I was in there, I could hear others screaming. One big guy just wouldn't fit in the box. I knew who he was by the sound of his voice. He was 6' 5", 250 pounds. They had to push and squeeze to get me into the box. I was 6' 2", 190 pounds at the time.

Another guy was claustrophobic. He was terrified of small places. He fought back, resisted.

It seemed we stayed in those boxes for hours.

To keep you from sleeping, they pounded on the boxes, just like they had pounded on our cell doors the night before. "Don't you sleep," was the mantra.

That kind of stuff went on for several days. I lost track of time, didn't know if it was day or night. Then, suddenly, our "captors" charged into the cells, put hoods over our heads and marched us outside.

When they told us to pull off the hoods and started playing the Star Spangled Banner while raising the U.S. flag there wasn't a dry eye to be found. It was one of the moments where your heart is racing. You can hear it pounding in your ears. You feel alive, almost as if for the first time.

It was a moment I'll never forget.

Is it true you met your wife while going to flying school?

I met my wife on the way to survival school actually. Our meeting each other was fate. Destiny, if you believe in that type of thing.

When I returned from Japan, I had the opportunity to stop over in Seattle, Washington before going to Fairchild AFB. I hadn't been home to the United States in nearly three years, so I wanted to have a bit of fun before going to survival school. That's when I met my wife.

We got married six months later and have been married ever since.

What was Germany like?

Germany is a beautiful country, so much to see and do. The people are wonderful. I love German food. I miss the German meats, cheeses, and breads. I miss going to Saturday market, traveling to castles on the weekends. Everything.

For most of our stay, my wife and I lived in the upstairs flat of a small brick home in Kaiserslautern, Germany. We were within walking distance of a pub, bakery and delicatessen. On the weekend, an ice cream man would come through the neighborhood. He served Italian ice cream. Tiny little scoops. Dozens of flavors. For 5 Deutsche Mark, about $3 US, at the time, you could get a large waffle cone filled with those deliciously small scoops.

The early 1990s were a wild time to be in Germany. We were there when the Kaiserslautern soccer team became champions in Germany. The day they won was wild. Everyone ran through the streets shouting and cheering.

We were there for the whole build-up before and during the Gulf War. With all the terrorist threats and whatnot, it was a scary time to be overseas. Travel was restricted. Every time you went on base, they checked the car from end to end for explosives.

My wife was alone in Germany most of that time, as I was sent to the Gulf War. After the war, things slowly came back to normal, but it was a hard time.

The Soviet Union dissolved. The Berlin wall fell. The divided Germanies became one country. We saw it all first hand, my wife and I. It was an exciting time, but a dangerous time. So much potential unrest yet everywhere everyone was so excited. It was a great time to be alive, to know democracy and freedom.

Tell me more about the food in Europe.

You haven't tasted real food and drink till you've been to Europe, and Germany in particular. The Germans really know how to celebrate, and food and drink is at the center of it all.

It seems every village in Germany brews its own beer, makes its own wine. There's always a festival celebrating something and Oktoberfest is the biggest celebration of them all.

For us, it was expensive eating out but we loved the food so much we couldn't resist. Schnitzel and brown gravy has been one of my favorite meals ever since.

Our landlord was one of the nicest guys. Brilliant too. He spoke seven languages. He'd invite my wife and me over about once a week or so.

Did you travel in Europe?

My wife and I traveled as much as we could. The first year was bliss. We couldn't afford much. The base had discounted bus tours. We could also drive places to see things. One of our most memorable drives took us along the Rhine River. We visited castles as we went.

The first castle I ever visited was Frankenstein Castle. I couldn't resist visiting that one.

One of the benefits (or drawbacks depending on viewpoint) of being on airborne duty is that I had to go on a lot of temporary duty assignments. Those assignments took me all over Germany. I also went to England, Belgium, and Scotland.

I spent two perfect weeks at Mildenhall Airbase, England. Whenever I had a chance, I'd get in a rented car and head to London or Cambridge with some of the other aircrew members. Had you been there at the time you would have found me skulking about in the university libraries and pubs. The libraries had such wonderful books, and the pubs were the best place to meet students attending university.

My only regret was that my wife couldn't join me. As a member of the aircrew, I flew to Mildenhall Airbase on our mission aircraft—the same plane we'd use in exercises on the temporary duty.

The one thing about England that I'll never forget is how friendly everyone is. I remember getting positively lost driving back from Cambridge one time. The person I was with suggested a just stop, roll down the window, and ask a passerby where to go. I laughed, said I knew where he tell me to go.

Boy was I wrong. The gentleman came straight over to the car and spent the next five minutes helping us find our way. He even let us use his pen so we could write down the directions.

How come you had to go to war?

When Iraq invaded Kuwait and the U.S. starting sending troops to the Middle East, I knew it might mean war. My father had been a freedom fighter in his native Hungary. My grandfather fought in the Spanish American War. I had relatives who served in World War I, World War II, the Korean War, and the Vietnam War.

I knew all about the Vietnam War and what a war in the Persian Gulf could mean, but I was never hesitant to do my duty. I volunteered to be among the first troops from our unit sent to the Gulf War and I was—even though the thought of war terrified me, and still does. Duty, honor, and country is the soldier's motto.

For me, it was a decision I had to make. It seemed the right choice then and it still does now. There are times in life when you have to make a choice. You can do nothing, or you can do something. I decided I wanted to do something.

Was it scary?

It wasn't only scary. It was terrifying. Words cannot describe or do justice to the horror of war. On my first mission, an Iraqi jet fighter launched against the plane I was flying in. I knew the capabilities of that fighter. I knew about the air-to-air missiles it carried. The gun canon used for strafing and close fighting.

That day I promised God that if he let me live I'd change my life. Do the things I said I would but never did. Become the person I should have become long ago.

That day was the first of many such. We had surface-to-air missiles launched against us several times. We had to fly through zones alive with anti-aircraft artillery fire.

Anyone who says they weren't terrified in such moments wouldn't be telling the truth. I was terrified. I still remember those dreadful times when I close my eyes sometimes.

But I wouldn't give those experiences back. I don't want to forget that time. Not even a moment of it. The Gulf War is a part of who I am. I earned the Distinguished Flying Cross, the United States of America's top flying honor, for my service.

Tell me about Hawaii.

My next assignment after the Gulf war was to Kunia Field Station, Hawaii. Kunia is an underground facility, carved under a hillside. During World War II, they made fighter aircraft in that facility. The fighter planes were flown out of Wheeler Army Air Station.

The Hawaiian Islands really are the pearls of the Pacific. It was a fortuitous assignment, more so than I knew at the time. My health deteriorated after the Gulf War. It was a secret I shared with few people. It wasn't manly to be sick that much. I didn't know what was happening to me. I only knew that I was taking sick frequently, but then in days or weeks I'd get better and everything would be fine for a while. I'd get strange rashes sometimes too. I remember getting a rash all around my eyes one time. That was the first symptom of the sickness for me.

My wife and I decided to have our first child around this time, and she suffered through three miscarriages. When she was carrying my son, she nearly lost him in the early weeks of pregnancy. I had to rush her to the hospital twice.

Years later I discovered that the thing I was experiencing had a name: Gulf War Syndrome. No one really understands it though. Some think it's a side effect of things soldiers were exposed to in the Gulf. Some think it's a side effect of the experimental drugs we took as a precaution against chemical and biological warfare agents. Some think it is the result of prolonged stress. Others think there's no such thing.

I personally think there is such a thing but I don't think we'll ever know for certain what causes it. I do believe, though, that if it weren't for Hawaii I wouldn't have made it through the years that followed the Gulf War. Some of my friends didn't make it.

But it wasn't a sad time on the whole. The weather in Hawaii is beautiful all year round. The sun and gentle climate are soothing. There is beauty everywhere. I was lucky to get stationed there. Someone really was watching over me and I do believe God answered my prayers.

During the same years that my health was privately falling apart, I got my "public" life together. The public and private me were two different people. I was afraid to share my secret pain. My career in the military was soaring. I earned several promotions, became our unit's technician of the year, and was on the road to Officer's Training School.

Academically, I was soaring too. Twice the military sent me to school, paying for my education. I went to six months of language classes at the University of Hawaii. I applied for and was accepted into the bootstrap program. I was one of two airmen selected for career and academic excellence, and given the opportunity to go to college full-time for a year.

The Dean of Hawaii Pacific University, the private college I attended, also granted me special permission to enter a dual-track degree program, allowing me to work on my master's degree at the same time I was completing my bachelor's degree.

The next year, I was the runner-up for class valedictorian and earned my bachelor's degree with top honors. The following year, I completed the master's program, earning my master's degree with distinction.

What made you want to get a degree, finally?

I made a decision during the Gulf War to turn my life around. Getting a degree was one of those things that I had said I would do but never had. I had tried before, but my heart was never in it. The problem is you need a degree to get ahead in life, and not only in whatever career you choose.

The extra years of education really do help mature a person. The rigor of study teaches more than is apparent. You also become more worldly wise, and hopefully more open-minded about the things you will see, do, and experience in life. You also have to learn discipline—you know: self-restraint, control, the ability to make the tough decisions. Things like not going out or watching television when you should study.

When I attended college classes in Japan, I was head of the class in Couch Potato 101. Let me tell you, it gets you nowhere. If I had completed my bachelor's degree in Japan when I started taking college classes, I would have been on the road to Officer's Training School ten years earlier than actually happened.

But I was too thick-skulled to understand. I thought that my job in the military was everything, that if I worked hard, I should be able to play hard. What I didn't understand was that as satisfying and challenging as the job was—and it was certainly both satisfying and challenging to direct intelligence operations—it was only a starting point in life and not an end point.

To get somewhere in life, I needed to drive there, myself. The gas for the car on that drive was a degree. It got me on the road to a better life.

Teacher's Classroom Guide: An Interview with Robert Stanek

Why did you leave the military?

The military is the best place for someone who has a dream or wants to find one. I can't imagine not having served, and it was truly a privilege.

Both of my degrees are in Computer Science. At the time, I was running the computer operations and analysis for our section, temporarily filling the position of a GS-15 who had returned to the states.

We were upgrading our entire operations, building a state of the art fiber optic network, backed by massive server arrays and high-power workstations. I was also training the new administration and analysis staff on everything from server installation to trouble shooting. It was a huge opportunity to put to use what I had learned in my degree programs.

One day near the end of the upgrade I came into the office and the GS-15's replacement was there. I had known that day would come. It was my job to help him transition. It was also the time when I had a decision to make: to stay in the military or to move on.

If I stayed in the military, I knew I wanted to become an officer. I had already completed my Officer's Training School package. I had full approval and was preparing for the training. Still it wasn't an easy decision, and one I didn't make until I had the completed package in my hand and was preparing to deliver it. In fact, I made the decision during the drive to drop off the package. I realized that as great as the military was and as exciting as it was to do what I did, it wasn't the best place for me.

When I made that decision, it was one of the hardest decisions I've ever had to make. Thinking about moving on, uprooting yourself and your family is terrifying. No one wants to start over in the middle of their life. It's like realizing that you've been standing in the wrong line for the past thirty years and now you've got to take a number and go to the end of a new line.

But that's exactly what I was doing when I decided to leave the military. I was starting over, moving back to square one, but I believed it was the right decision—and I still do.

There are times in life when you have to make a decision to move on or to keep doing what you are doing. The hardest, toughest, yet truest decision might be to move on, but you have to be willing to remake yourself, to put in the same long hours you did when you were just starting out, and you have to believe that you can achieve what you set out to achieve.

Writing Career

When did you first start writing fiction?

For years, I had been thinking of a book with the characters of Vilmos, Adrina, and Seth. I had this notion of three characters with very different backgrounds that would band together to stop a coming darkness.

Shortly after being stationed in Japan in 1986, I was sitting alone in my barracks room. I had just worked the midnight shift and I couldn't sleep. I turned on the computer, an Amiga 500, that I had bought my senior year of high school.

I started out with the intention of writing a letter home, but when I turned on the computer I got sidetracked. After a time, I was just sitting there staring at the blank screen. The word processor was started. The blank page and the blinking cursor seemed an invitation. For some reason, I don't know why, an image of Princess Adrina came into my mind's eye. She was standing atop a wall, staring out into the world. I started typing, and the words just came:

> Summer must surely be at an end, Adrina surmised, for the breeze came from the North and not from the direction of the West Deep.

I stopped there. Suddenly, all the ideas I had been thinking about for years were coming together in my mind. I turned away from the keyboard, grabbed a notebook and pen. I wrote down all my thoughts, started putting the disconnected pieces together. Within several weeks, I filled the notebook and started another. The ideas kept flowing.

I knew almost immediately that the story I had to tell couldn't be told in a single book. I was writing the background history and story ideas for a series of books, and one idea in particular stuck in my mind: the notion of a world where the history was subject to interpretation. There are two sides to every story, and I knew that the world I was inventing had to have two sets of histories.

I spent the next three years writing the history and the stories. I finished writing the first book and hundreds of pages of history before I showed anyone what I'd written.

When did you first try to get published?

I'd been tinkering with writing for many years. I'd written stories, but never anything longer than a few pages. I'd never tried to get any of my stories published and the idea of getting published never crossed my mind when I started writing about Adrina and her friends.

Years passed. I kept writing, and by the early 1990s I had several completed manuscripts, including *Magic Lands: Journey Beyond the Beyond*, and many hundreds of pages of history for the world I called *Ruin Mist*. It wasn't until the Persian Gulf War that I found focus in my life, however. My wife played a large part in that, but the war also.

The war gave me time to retrospect on what I'd accomplished in my life, and up until that time, it wasn't much. I had wasted my talents. I hadn't done anything I said I was going to do with my life.

I subscribed to *Writer's Digest* for the first time and began reading books on how to get published. In 1991, after reading about an essay contest, I submitted a story and won.

Winning the contest gave me the courage to write a proposal that I sent to publishers, but I think most of the publishers who received the proposal dismissed it offhand. I was an unknown, unpublished writer who was trying to sell a series of books. I didn't have an agent, either.

The inevitable rejections didn't dissuade me from continuing; they only strengthened my resolve. I studied the industry more, tried to correspond with writers I respected, like it says in some of the books on getting published.

Let me tell you though, firsthand, that chivalry is dead. None of the writers I wrote for advice ever wrote back.

In 1993, I sent out very selective query letters to individual publishers. I got strong interest from Tor. An editor asked for the complete manuscript and we started corresponding. But Tor ultimately decided to not to publish, and I kept trudging on.

Teacher's Classroom Guide: An Interview with Robert Stanek

The next submission got a direct response from the executive editor. The editor stated, "The fantasy world you have created is truly wonderful and rich. Your characters seem real and full of life." The story I created wasn't right for the publisher's line of books, however. I quickly discovered that other publishers weren't sure how to fit the book in their list either.

In fantasy books, epic quests like Terry Brook's *Shannara* were what publishers were publishing and readers were buying. Publishers had no idea what to do with the type of story I had written.

The books at their heart were a story of intrigue between two powerful families: the House of Alder and the House of Tyr'anth. Epic quests were a part of the story, but they weren't *the* story.

In some versions of the work, I submitted the story of Adrina, Vilmos, and Seth as separate chapters. Chapter 1 began Adrina's story. Chapter 2, Vilmos'. Chapter 3, Seth's. Chapter 4 continued Adrina's story, Chapter 5 Vilmos' and so on. I was told that approach would never sell. No one would ever buy a book where the story switched to a different character every chapter. But if you read current fiction you know how wrong they were about that.

Based on the strong disapproval of the idea, I revised my manuscripts and tried different approaches. Eventually though, I ended up right where I started, which was frustrating.

By 1995, I was just about to give up the dream of getting published when I got my first big break: I sold an editor on a proposal for a technical how-to book—something I knew very well. That led to my career as a technical how-to writer.

What happened after your first book was published?

The publisher I was working with really liked that book. Before it was published, I was already contracted to write a second book. By the time the first book was in stores, I was writing the second book. At the time, 1995, I was in the military, completing my degree, and trying to meet the deadlines for the second book—any one of which was a full-time job by itself.

I had a three-year-old running around the house and we didn't have a room where I could work in private. I set up my desk in the living room, a few feet from the TV. I adapted, blocked out the distractions and got the work done. Looking back, the best part of it all was that I was surrounded by family at that stressful time.

In 1996, I decided not to pursue a career as a military officer and got out of the Air Force. At the same time, my publisher was adapting my bestselling how-to book and I was writing additional materials for a professional reference edition.

The publisher also packaged that edition with software titles, creating *The Professional Web Design Kit* and *The Web Publishing Electronic Resource Kit*.

What is *Magic Lands* about?

Magic Lands is the story of Ray. It details his adventures to the place lost and deep, and beyond. The story begins with Ray setting out from his home village to find the place lost and deep. He believes that if he is successful in reaching this place it will prove that he is no longer a child. What Ray doesn't understand is that the quest really isn't about finding the place lost and deep so much as it is about finding himself on the journey.

The journey to the place lost and deep exposes him to the real world—a world full of danger. The things he encounters along the way help him learn about himself, and transition from childhood to adolescence. In a way, the journey itself represents his loss of innocence, his transition from childhood.

What about the imagery in the story?

I've created a world where there is water everywhere, populated it with strange creatures, and even stranger notions. The plants and animals in this world are very different from those in our world. The so-called houses, avenues and rooftops that Ray goes along float on top of the water, and this means the ground that Ray walks on moves and shifts beneath his feet.

Ray has never been on solid ground. He is in fact afraid of what he calls the stone land—a place where it is rumored that the ground doesn't move beneath one's feet.

Ray, in fact, has a lot of prejudices and preconceptions about the world around him.

Prejudice and preconception seem to be themes in your work.

In a way, this is true. Prejudice and preconception are themes in my *Ruin Mist* books, and they are themes in *Magic Lands* as well. I think prejudice and preconception are a part of our society. I think everyone has prejudices and preconceptions—whether we realize it or not—and these notions aren't just about different peoples. They can be about places and things too. In the story Ray has very distinct preconceptions about his world. These preconceptions color the way he sees the world and himself.

Tell us about the bulls and the slithers.

The water-logged world in which Ray lives is populated by a variety of troublesome creatures. As I said previously, it is a dangerous world. Not only are the waters full of black suckers that get in places you'd least expect and suck your blood, they are also home to bulls and slithers.

Bulls are large crocodile-like creatures that have great big jaws full of sharp teeth and long tails that lash out at you. In the story, bulls always lurk just out of eyesight to catch Ray if he falters. Slithers are enormous snake-like creatures with fangs that hide in the water or in the undergrowth, waiting to strike.

Are other *Magic Lands* books planned?

I've always thought of *Magic Lands* as a series of books rather than a single book. The first book is about Ray's coming of age. The second book, called *Magic Lands: In the Stone Land*, is about the growing friendship between Ray and Kerry and the challenges they face as they set out to discover the world around them. Ray and Kerry's relationship—a friendship between two people with very different backgrounds—is at the heart of the story, and the things they encounter as they explore the Stone Land tests the bonds and bounds of their friendship.

Review Questions

Review Questions for Discussion: Chapter 1

1. How did Ray feel about proving himself as a man? Why do you think he feels this way? (He feels determined and prepared to overcome any obstacle in his path. He wants to prove himself and become a man.)

2. Whose words rang through Ray's thoughts during many events in this chapter? Why are these words so important to Ray and his journey? (The words of the Village Smoot. The words are meant to help guide Ray.)

3. Who did it seem Ray was destined to meet? How did he feel about meeting him/her? (Ray thinks it is inevitable that he will meet the wizard. He feels he does not want to meet him.)

4. What convinced the elders it was time for Ray to leave? (Ray's dreams of the wizard and the mountain in addition to Tall's painting.)

5. What was the name of the creature that chased Ray? Why do you think Old Bull is chasing Ray. (Old Bull. At this point in the story, it seems Old Bull wants to catch and perhaps eat Ray.)

6. What was the question troubling Ray during his journey? Why was this question important? (Whether he would choose a slither or bull when the time came. The choosing was very important because it represents a key part of Ray's journey to manhood. The companion he chooses will also be with him for life.)

7. Why do you think Ray decided not to go to Second Village? (Probably because he feared the sights of home and comfort would make him decide not to continue on his journey.)

8. Which of his friends did Ray envy? Why? (He envied Tall. Probably because Tall was safe in the village and still waiting to start his journey.)

Teacher's Classroom Guide: Review Questions

Review Questions for Discussion: Chapters 2-3

Chapter 2

1. What saved Ray from his encounter with the young bull? Why do you think this happened? (Old Bull's interference saved Ray. At this point in the story, it seems Old Bull wants Ray for his own.)

2. What made Ray sick and queasy? Why? (The suckers. He doesn't like suckers or the way they attach themselves to skin.)

3. What did Ray put around him when he slept and how did he sleep? Why did he sleep this way? (He used some leaves of the stinging to help protect him while he slept. He slept with his eyes open, allowing anything his eyes saw to be seen by him in the form of a dream, so he could escape from harm if needed.)

4. What events made Ray one step closer to becoming a man? (Finding the place lost and deep, and surviving an encounter with a bull.)

Chapter 3

1. What doubts did not being able to choose his companion bring to Ray? (Doubts of whether or not he was ready and worthy to prove himself.)

2 What did Ray do to the Arbor Trees? Why did he do this? (He put his mark on them. It was part of his journey to show he had been to the place lost and deep, and to prove he was a man.)

3. What choice did Ray finally make for a companion? How did he get the creature? (Ray chose a slither. He stuck his hand into a nest to receive an egg.)

4. Where did he put the companion? (The container he had made.)

Teacher's Classroom Guide: Review Questions

Review Questions for Discussion: Chapters 4-5

Chapter 4

1. What did Ray feel tempted to do with the egg? Why do you think he felt this way? (He wanted to crack the egg open. He was impatient and wanted to see his companion.)

2. What was it forbidden to do in Ray's village? Why? (It was forbidden to speak of another's dream quest. Probably because the journey was a personal experience meant to be private.)

3. Why did Ray choose to continue on with his quest? Why was this decision important? (He decided to continue to prove himself not only to the villagers but also to himself. It showed he was making able to make decisions on his own and that he was maturing.)

4. What was wrong about Ray's dream of Tall? (The figure had deep set eyes. Tall didn't.)

5. What attacked Ray while he rested? (A slither. He thought it was a bull but it wasn't.)

Chapter 5

1. Who did Ray dream about? Why do you think he had this dream? (Ray had a dream about the wizard. He most likely had this dream because his quest wasn't complete as he may have thought after reaching the place lost and deep, and finding his companion.)

2. What did Ray do when the slither hatched? (He realized he forgot to prepare and frightened the slither.)

3. What caused Ray to get very worried and despair? (He thought his companion left him, which would have caused him to fail a vital part of his journey.)

4. How did Ray come about the black leaf? (Tall gave it to him the day Keene and Ephramme were picked instead of him and Tall.)

Teacher's Classroom Guide: Review Questions

Review Questions for Discussion: Chapters 6-7

Chapter 6

1. How did the slither react to the names Ray whispered to it? (It did not respond until Ray said its name would be True.)

2. Why did True run to the wet? (Because it was hungry and wished to eat.)

3. Why did Ray want to chase the strangers away? Was his thinking accurate? Or was there something wrong about his way of thinking? (He felt the strangers were stealing from his land. His thinking is clouded by his preconceptions that the In is only for his people.)

4. What happened to Old Bull? Who did this to him? (Old Bull was killed by Braddick.)

5. How did Ray feel about Old Bull's fate at the hands of the strangers? (He felt saddened for the loss of a valiant foe who had pushed him beyond his limits and angered at the loss of a valiant creature by the hands of the minions of the wizard.)

Chapter 7

1. What was the other name Ray called the Out? Why do you think he called it this? (The stone land. Because the ground was solid and did not move beneath your feet.)

2. Who visited Ray near the stone land? Why? (The village smoot visited Ray. The smoot wanted to speak with Ray about the rest of his journey.)

3. What doubts did the arrival of the visitor bring to Ray? Was Ray right? (He thought the smoot's arrival meant his journey was at an end. Ray was wrong. His journey wasn't over.)

4. What confirmation did the stranger make? Why was this important? (The smoot told Ray he had proved himself a man. It meant an important part of his vision quest was completed.)

Review Questions for Discussion: Chapters 8-9

Chapter 8

1. What was the name of the wizard's city? (The city is named Adalayia.)

2. What did Kerry do to the trees after they gave her their fruit? (She sang to them, thanking them for their offering.)

3. Who screeched at Kerry? (Her companion, Waring.)

4. What did Kerry use to respond to the screech? Why did she do this? (She used a lure because she wanted to catch Waring.)

Chapter 9

1. Who or what attempted to attack Kerry? (A bull tried to attack Kerry.)

2. What did Ray do to stop the attack? Why did he do this? Do you think he was right in acting the way he did? (Ray attacked the bull until it retreated. He didn't want Kerry to get hurt. Although he was interfering with the natural order, he was right to do so because Kerry didn't know about the dangerous creatures in Ray's world.)

3. What did Kerry believe the wizard received his power from? (The heads of mysterious beasts mounted on walls in his domain.)

4. Why did Kerry think Ray was a barbarian? (He did not know of the falling off and he showed no fear of them.)

Teacher's Classroom Guide: Review Questions

Review Questions for Discussion: Chapters 10-11

Chapter 10

1. What was Kerry worried about? (Waring's disappearance.)

2. What did Stirling do that cost him his life? (He didn't pay the wizard's taxes.)

3. Why did Kerry dislike True? (She thought it was dangerous and pictured it strangling her in her dreams.)

4. What did Ray want to show Kerry? Why? (Rain. Kerry had never seen rain before and Ray wanted to show it to her.)

5. What did Ray think Waring was? What is Waring? (Ray thought Waring was an insect. Waring is a winged beast.)

Chapter 11

1. Why did Ray have to hide? (Kerry wanted him to be hidden from the soldiers. She was afraid for his safety.)

2. Why did the soldiers break Kerry's furniture? (To punish her for not opening the door the first time they asked her to.)

3. How did Kerry prepare the trees so they could bear extra fruit? (She applied a full day's dosage of life liquid and asked them to bear extra fruit for her.)

4. What were the two reasons she did not want to leave her house? (Her promise to Stirling and because she needed to tend to Waring.)

Teacher's Classroom Guide: Review Questions

Review Questions for Discussion: Chapter 12

1. What did Kerry do when she awoke? Why did she do this? (She tried to find Waring. She was worried about him.)

2. Where did Ray decide they were going to go? Why did he decide this? (He decided they were going to go to Adalayia. He decided this because it is what he saw in his dreams and he was convinced this is what he must do to continue his quest.)

3. Who scratched at the door of Kerry's home? What was Ray's first reaction to this person or creature? (Waring scratched at the door. Ray took an instant liking to Waring, and Waring liked Ray as well.)

4. What did Ray tell Kerry about home? What do you think he meant by this? (He told her home was where and what they make it. He meant home can be anywhere as long as you believe in your heart.)

5. What did Ray dream of? Why did he tell Kerry about this dream? (He had a dream in which he and Kerry were in the land beyond the beyond. He wanted her to see what he saw and to convince her they were making the right decision.)

6. What did Kerry tell to her trees that she did not tell Ray? (That she would be back.)

7. Where were Ray and Kerry going? Do you think they made the right choice? (They were going to Adalayia and beyond. It seems they made the right decision given the circumstances and the fact that Ray's still had much further to go to complete his quest.)

Quizzes

Quiz!: Chapter 1

1. How did Ray feel about proving himself as a man? Why do you think he feels this way?
_____
_____

2. Whose words rang through Ray's thoughts during many events in this chapter? Why are these words so important to Ray and his journey?
_____
_____

3. Who did it seem Ray was destined to meet? How did he feel about meeting him/her?
_____
_____

4. What convinced the elders it was time for Ray to leave?
_____

5. What was the name of the creature chasing Ray? Why do you think Old Bull chases Ray?
_____
_____

6. What was the question troubling Ray? Why was this question important?
_____
_____

7. Why do you think Ray decided not to go to Second Village?
_____
_____

8. Which of his friends did Ray envy? Why?
_____
_____

Teacher's Classroom Guide: Quizzes

Quiz!: Chapter 2

1. What saved Ray from his encounter with the young bull? Why do you think this happened?

_____
_____
_____
_____

2. What made Ray sick and queasy? Why?

_____
_____

3. What did Ray put around him when he slept and how did he sleep? Why did he sleep this way?

_____
_____
_____
_____

4. What events made Ray one step closer to becoming a man?

_____
_____

Teacher's Classroom Guide: Quizzes

Quiz!: Chapter 3

1. What doubts did not being able to choose his companion bring to Ray?
_____
_____

2 What did Ray do to the Arbor Trees? Why did he do this?
_____
_____
_____

3. What choice did Ray finally make for a companion? How did he get the creature?
_____
_____
_____

4. Where did he put the companion? What did he keep the companion in?
_____
_____

Quiz!: Chapter 4

1. What did Ray feel tempted to do with the egg? Why do you think he felt this way?

2. What was it forbidden to do in Ray's village? Why?

3. Why did Ray choose to continue on with his quest? Why was this decision important?

4. What was wrong about Ray's dream of Tall?

5. What attacked Ray while he rested?

Teacher's Classroom Guide: Quizzes

Quiz!: Chapter 5

1. Who did Ray dream about? Why do you think he had this dream?
_____
_____
_____
_____

2. What did Ray do when the slither hatched?
_____
_____
_____
_____

3. What caused Ray to get very worried and despair?
_____
_____

4. How did Ray come about the black leaf?
_____
_____

Quiz!: Chapter 6

1. What soothed Ray's hard feelings?

2. How did the slither react to the names Ray whispered to it?

3. Why did True run to the wet?

4. Why did Ray want to chase the strangers away? Was his thinking accurate? Or was there something wrong about his way of thinking?

5. What happened to Old Bull? Who did this to him?

6. How did Ray feel about Old Bull's fate at the hands of the strangers?

Teacher's Classroom Guide: Quizzes

Quiz!: Chapter 7

1. What was the other name Ray called the Out? Why do you think he called it this?
_____
_____

2. Who visited Ray near the stone land? Why?
_____
_____
_____
_____

3. What doubts did the arrival of the visitor bring to Ray? Was Ray right or wrong?
_____
_____
_____
_____

4. What confirmation did the stranger make? Why was this important?
_____
_____
_____
_____

Teacher's Classroom Guide: Quizzes

Quiz!: Chapter 8

1. What was the name of the wizard's city?

2. What did Kerry do to the trees after they gave her their fruit? Why did she do this?

3. Who screeched at Kerry?

4. What did Kerry use to respond to the screech? Why did she do this?

Teacher's Classroom Guide: Quizzes

Quiz!: Chapter 9

1. Who or what attempted to attack Kerry?
_____
_____

2. What did Ray do to stop the attack? Why did he do this? Do you think he was right in acting the way he did?
_____
_____
_____
_____

3. What did Kerry believe the wizard received his power from?
_____
_____

4. Why did Kerry think Ray was a barbarian?
_____
_____
_____
_____

Teacher's Classroom Guide: Quizzes

Quiz!: Chapter 10

1. What was Kerry worried about?
_____
_____

2. What did Stirling do that cost him his life?
_____
_____

3. Why did Kerry dislike True?
_____
_____

4. What did Ray want to show Kerry? Why?
_____
_____

5. What did Ray think Waring was? What is Waring?
_____
_____

Teacher's Classroom Guide: Quizzes

Quiz!: Chapter 11

1. Why did Ray have to hide?
_____
_____

2. Why did the soldiers break Kerry's furniture?
_____
_____

3. How did Kerry prepare the trees so they could bear extra fruit?
_____
_____

4. What were the two reasons she did not want to leave her house?
_____
_____
_____
_____

Teacher's Classroom Guide: Quizzes

Quiz!: Chapter 12

1. What did Kerry do when she awoke? Why did she do this?

2. Where did Ray decide they were going to go? Why did he decide this?

3. Who scratched at the door of Kerry's home? What was Ray's first reaction to this person or creature?

4. What did Ray tell Kerry about home? What do you think he meant by this?

5. What did Ray dream of? Why did he tell Kerry about this dream?

6. What did Kerry tell to her trees that she did not tell Ray?

7. Where were Ray and Kerry going? Do you think they made the right choice?

Post-Reading & Writing Activities

Write a Journal!

Writing Activity:

Write a journal entry from either Ray's or Kerry's point of view describing their thoughts pertaining to the other character. Be creative, in depth, and descriptive in your writing.

Teacher's Classroom Guide: Post-Reading Activities

What's the main idea?

Writing Activity:

Select four chapters from the book and describe why you think the author named the titles the way he did. Use specific examples from the book to explain your answer. Be as detailed as possible.

Find the Meaning

Writing Activity:

During the story the author uses unorthodox terms to describe some objects in his novel. Discuss some of these terms and what you think they are and why. Use specific examples from the book to back up your statements. Be as detailed as possible.

_____
_____
_____
_____
_____
_____
_____
_____
_____
_____
_____
_____
_____
_____
_____
_____
_____
_____
_____
_____
_____

Put Yourself in Ray's Place

Writing Activity:

Imagine you are Ray. Discuss how you would have handled the event in which Ray sees the strangers kill Old Bull. Write about what you would have done and the possible outcomes of your actions. Share your ideas with your class. Be factual, descriptive, and creative with your work.

Teacher's Classroom Guide: Post-Reading Activities

What's So Special About Ray's Quest

Writing Activity:

In the novel Ray sets out on a journey. Write about why you think he does this, the purpose of his quest, and why he collected various items along the way. Do you think his knowledge of herb lore assisted him in his quest? Explain your answers. Utilize your creative thinking skills. Be original!

_____
_____
_____
_____
_____
_____
_____
_____
_____
_____
_____
_____
_____
_____
_____
_____
_____
_____
_____
_____

Teacher's Classroom Guide: Post-Reading Activities

Be the Character!

Writing Activity:

Pick Ray, Kerry, True, or Waring. Imagine they are living in your world. Then pick a place where they will live in your world and describe how they would feel and also what they would think, see, and hear. Try to describe everyday objects as if you do not know what they are. For example, an apple could be described as a shiny red fruit as opposed to just calling it an apple. Pick a creative style to mirror their feelings and thoughts.

Teacher's Classroom Guide: Post-Reading Activities

What's in a Personality?

Writing Activity:

Compare and contrast the personalities of Kerry and Ray. Write about their personalities as well as physical attributes. Expand upon your thoughts and create an interesting and factual paper.

All About Friends

Writing Activity:

Ray was away from his village, possibly for the first time alone. What do you think he felt when he thought about his friends? Discuss how you think he felt and then incorporate this into a paper describing your thoughts about whether or not you think his journey would have been different if he took Tall or another of his friends with him. Be specific and provide reasons and examples which reflect your thinking.

_____
_____
_____
_____
_____
_____
_____
_____
_____
_____
_____
_____
_____
_____
_____
_____
_____
_____
_____
_____

Teacher's Classroom Guide: Post-Reading Activities

Ray's Vision Quest

Writing Activity:

Think carefully about Ray's journey. The author based it upon an event still used in some cultures today. Discuss what you think the author based Ray's journey on, and state why you think this way.

Teacher's Classroom Guide: Post-Reading Activities

Oh no the Palisades!

Writing Activity:

After reading this book, why do you think the author included a definition of a palisade in the beginning of the story? Be specific and include your reasoning.

Teacher's Classroom Guide: Post-Reading Activities

You Choose the Companion!

Writing Activity:

Do you think Ray made the right choice when he picked a slither instead of a bull? What companion would you have chosen? Provide your reasoning, details, and if you think the bull would have made a better companion explain why, or if you think the slither is the better choice, explain why.

_____
_____
_____
_____
_____
_____
_____
_____
_____
_____
_____
_____
_____
_____
_____
_____
_____
_____
_____
_____

Teacher's Classroom Guide: Post-Reading Activities

The Place Lost and Deep

Writing Activity:

In the novel, what changed about how Ray marked the trees? Why do you think he changed his mark? Also, why did he not mark the third tree? Incorporate these answers into a detailed and thoughtful essay.

_____
_____
_____
_____
_____
_____
_____
_____
_____
_____
_____
_____
_____
_____
_____
_____
_____
_____
_____
_____

Teacher's Classroom Guide: Post-Reading Activities

Friend or Adversary?

Writing Activity:

After reading this book, thinking about it clearly, and reviewing the smoot's words, why do you think Old Bull really followed Ray? Write a detailed explanation of your thinking. Remember, creativity, constant focus upon quality, and hard work will create a high quality paper.

_____
_____
_____
_____
_____
_____
_____
_____
_____
_____
_____
_____
_____
_____
_____
_____
_____
_____
_____
_____

Teacher's Classroom Guide: Post-Reading Activities

Into the Beyond

Writing Activity:

During the last few pages of this novel, Ray harbored some optimistic thoughts pertaining to reaching his goal of finding Frething and returning to tell his friends with Kerry at his side. Write about whether or not you think Ray and Kerry will reach Frething and return. Also write about the hardships you think they will face. What do you think they will find in Frething? Or do you think they will fail in the attempt? Incorporate all these thoughts into a form of writing, be it essay, a short story chronicling the events, or some other form of expressing your thoughts. Fine tune your imaginative and writing skills to develop a creative and descriptive project.

Culminating Project for Magic Lands

Culminating Project For Magic Lands

After reading, reviewing, and completing the post reading activities, one final test remains. To leave a lasting impression of *Magic Lands* upon its readers, a final culminating project was created. From each section, pick one project and complete it along with your selections from the other sections. The time frame of this project should be discussed in class. Make sure you choose the projects you can most expand upon, and not the easiest projects. Enhanced quality, depth of content and hard work will result in an impressive final project.

Section 1

Every question should be answered in essay format with at least five paragraphs. For higher quality, question three should also be answered in paragraph format even though it says to make a list.

1. Pick the three most important events in the novel. Write a summary of these events and then write about how you would have handled the events as opposed to how Ray did.

2. Think carefully about all the lessons Ray learned during his travels. Pick what you think is the most important lesson he learned and write about how he learned the lesson, how the lesson changed him, and why you think this is an important lesson. Persuasiveness and examples from the story should lead to higher quality work.

3. Revisit the thoughts you have about Ray's choice of companion. List the pros and cons of choosing a slither in a creative and factual way. Perhaps putting your thoughts in paragraph form instead of a list would prove to be a more beneficial and challenging activity.

4. During the novel, when Ray was in danger, Old Bull came to his rescue many times. Do you think Old Bull rescued him just so he could hunt Ray or do you think there was some other reasoning? Perhaps your thoughts on the post reading activity entitled "Friend or Adversary?" could aid your reasoning.

5. Do you think Ray's journey would have been different if he did not have a staff? Do you think that it would have been different? Do you think Ray possibly would not have survived? Write about three events in which Ray's staff helped immensely.

Teacher's Classroom Guide: Post-Reading Activities

Section 2

Section 2 questions can be answered using a single paragraph, but may be extended beyond that by students seeking an extra challenge.

1. What do you think the smoot meant by "Go until you think you can't go any more, and then go just a little bit more." How did these words help Ray?

2. Why do you think Waring called to Kerry when she first arrived at her cottage and then went away?

3. How did Ray and Kerry react to each other at first? Why did they act this way?

4. What did Ray do to ease the process of True's shedding? Explain.

Section 3

Section three focuses upon individual creativity. For this reason, it is up to students to come up with their own way of completing these projects. To quote a teacher, and Albert Einstein, "Imagination is more important than knowledge."

1. Draw a detailed picture of an event in the story, or one of Ray's dreams, include a caption that states why you picked the event or dream.

2. Write an imaginative short story chronicling Ray and Kerry's adventures after the novel ends. Discuss with your teacher about how long it should be.

3. Imagine Ray returns to the place where Old Bull was killed. Draw a picture of and describe in words a monument he would build to let the world know what a formidable and magnificent creature Old Bull was.

4. Create your own project that demonstrates your knowledge of *Magic Lands*.

Keeper Martin's Tales

The Kingdoms & the Elves of the Reaches
Inside you'll discover the breathtaking world of Ruin Mist where the mystical and the magical abound, and you'll fall in love with a boy who would become a mage, a princess who is just now seeing the world around her, a warrior elf who undertakes an epic journey, and their friends.

The Kingdoms & the Elves of the Reaches 2
Adrina, Emel, Vilmos, Galan and Seth must survive the greatest challenge Great Kingdom has faced in hundreds of years: the dissolution of the Kingdom Alliance and the battle to save Quashan'. Survival in a changing world depends on their ability to adapt and if they fail, their world and everything they believe in will perish.

The Kingdoms & the Elves of the Reaches 3 & 4
Adrina, Emel, Vilmos, Galan and Seth face even greater challenges as their world is transformed. Vilmos, in his quest to become the first human magus in a thousand years, must control the darkness within him. Adrina must accept her place and work together with Emel to help the elves make their plea to Great Kingdom's council. What happens along the way will amaze you.

In the Service of Dragons

The direct continuation of The Kingdoms & the Elves of the Reaches!

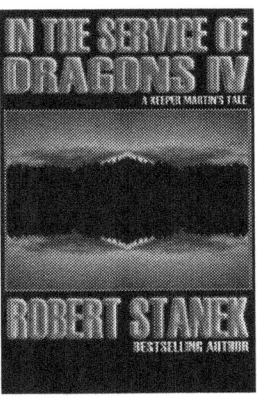

Ruin Mist Tales

For every fantastic story you'll ever find there are often other stories that retell the adventures from different points of view—so why should it be any different in Ruin Mist? Join us now as we walk the dark path through the chronicles of Ruin Mist. Discover new secrets, new dangers, new visions and new realities!

Magic Lands

Following the village elder's advice, Ray leaves his home village, setting out for the place lost and deep where he will find a companion for his journey to the stone land and where he will discover that there is no easy path from childhood to manhood. "Beware lashing tail and gnashing teeth," the village elder warns him, "and if Old Bull doesn't get you, Mother Slither surely will."

Thank you for your purchase! Please visit www.tvpress.com and www.robertstanek.com on the Internet for more information on Robert Stanek and his books.

www.ingramcontent.com/pod-product-compliance
Lightning Source LLC
Chambersburg PA
CBHW051419070526
44584CB00023B/3497